BADGER ASSEMBLY STORIES

WITH GLOBAL ISSUES THEMES

Ages 5–7

Sally Maynard, Andy and Barbara Seed

Badger Publishing
15 Wedgwood Gate, Pin Green Industrial Estate, Stevenage, Hertfordshire SG1 4SU
Telephone: 01438 356907 Fax: 01438 747015

Cover photograph: Educational Solutions Ltd

Once it has been purchased, you may copy this book freely for use in your school. The pages in this book are copyright, but copies may be made without fees or prior permission provided that these copies are used only by the institution which purchased the book. For copying in any other circumstances, prior written consent must be obtained from the publisher.

INTRODUCTION

There are 30 assemblies for children aged 5–7 in this book, all with Global Issues themes. Each assembly begins with an introduction and then a main presentation, usually given by the teacher. There are both interactive and non-interactive follow-up ideas and every assembly concludes with an optional reflection or prayer.

The assemblies use a wide range of stimulus material:
- Original stories
- 'True life' stories: factual accounts of people's lives
- Factual accounts of events
- Information, e.g. about charities, pressure groups and voluntary organisations
- Mini drama sketches for children to perform, with play scripts

There is a link to the most relevant RE, Citizenship and Geography unit from the QCA Scheme of Work and Programmes of Study in each assembly.

Follow-up

Each assembly presentation is followed by suggestions for interaction to involve the audience in the assembly and to reinforce learning.

Interactive follow-up activities include:
- Closed and open questions
- Active response, e.g. vote, hands up, thumbs up or down, giving scores
- Quizzes
- Use of volunteers to assist at the front
- Discussion

Non-interactive follow-up suggestions include: a summary of the story; points to think about; reflection and prayer.

Using the material

The assemblies in the book are designed to be used flexibly: it is intended that teachers select the most appropriate follow-up activities and questions from the range provided in order to meet the needs of the children present. The basic core presentation of each assembly may also be adapted to suit the school, of course, and may be used, for example, in circle time as the basis for role-play or other drama or for classroom discussion.

Questions to stimulate response from the children might include:
- What might it feel like to be in this situation?
- Have you experienced a situation like this in real life?
- Why did the characters do what they did?
- Were they right/wrong?
- What do you think you could do about this?

What makes a successful assembly?

Good preparation is essential, particularly if drama is involved.

Other key pointers:
- Use of props or a visual focus (suggestions are included in the book; don't forget an OHP or data projector can be used if you can't find the object suggested).
- Relate the contents of the assembly to activities going on in the school or community.
- Interactivity: music, songs, drama or any kind of audience participation generates interest.
- Use the story or presentation to make a single clear learning point, which can be reinforced in the reflection or prayer at the end of the assembly.

Contents

		Page
1.	Racism	5
2.	Pollution Solution!	8
3.	Recycling	12
4.	A Local Citizen is a Global Citizen	15
5.	Fairtrade	19
6.	Children's Rights	23
7.	Hunger	26
8.	Peace and Conflict	29
9.	Be Cool, Save our Fuel!	32
10.	Animals in Danger 1: Dolphins	36
11.	Animals in Danger 2: Tibetan Antelopes	39
12.	Animals in Danger 3: The Giant Panda	42
13.	Animals in Danger 4: Tigers	45
14.	Animals in Danger 5: The Green Sea Turtle	49
15.	Animals in Danger 6: The Blue Whale	53
16.	Farming	56
17.	Health	59
18.	We're all Special (Image)	62
19.	Looking after the Environment: Litter Bug	65
20.	Law and Order	69
21.	Global Warming	73
22.	Need and Want	76
23.	Homelessness	80
24.	Water	83
25.	Keeping safe in the sun	86

1 Racism

Objective
For children to value and respect others as equal and different and for them to be aware of and have pride in their own individuality.

Links
Citizenship
2a: to reflect on spiritual, moral, social and cultural issues using imagination to understand other people's experiences
2b: to realise the consequences of anti-social and aggressive behaviours, such as bullying and racism, on individuals and communities

Props
A wig which is brightly coloured!
Drawings of people with big ears, big noses, different coloured hair.

Introduction

(Put the wig on before you come into the assembly so that the children can see it when they arrive. Children will undoubtedly start laughing, when they settle down, start the assembly.) Has anyone noticed anything different about me today? *(Invite responses.)* You're right, my hair's different. Do you like it? No? *(look sad)* I though it suited me rather well. *(look sadder)* I didn't think people would laugh at me just because my hair was a different colour. *(pause)* Now, I know that you were laughing because bright (green) isn't the best colour for a wig and, let's face it, I look funny! *(Take wig off.)* But today we're going to think about people who are treated differently or badly for silly reasons.

Story: The Boy with the bright yellow socks
Once there was a very clever little boy, and he was looking forward very much to starting his new school. On the morning of his first day, his mother took him to his class, kissed him and told him that she would come back for him at lunch-time. The little boy looked around him at all the interesting things there were to play with and learn about. He saw two boys who were looking at a game on one of the computers. 'Hello,' he said, 'can I play too?'

One of the boys turned round, looked at the little boy and then nudged his friend. They both started laughing at him. 'Look at your socks,' one of them said. 'They're bright yellow!' And they laughed and laughed, then turned round and carried on with their game. The little boy felt hurt and bewildered. He loved his yellow socks. Then he noticed that a lot of the children were looking at him and staring. Some of them were laughing and some of them were pointing. The little boy thought that he was going to cry and started towards the door. Just then the classroom door opened and another boy came in.

The little boy braced himself for some more pointing and laughing but the new boy said to him, 'Hello, do you want to play with me?' The little boy was amazed and delighted. So he said, 'Yes please!' Off they went and got out the Lego and began playing together very happily. After a while, the two boys on the computer went over and asked if they could play Lego too. When they saw the four boys playing together, the other children began to feel very uncomfortable and realized that they had been very unfair in treating the little boy differently just because he was wearing bright yellow socks. What do you think?

INTERACTIVE FOLLOW-UP

Questions
1) What was the little boy looking forward to? *(his first day at school)*
2) What did he notice when he first went in the classroom? *(all the interesting things there were to play with and to learn about)*
3) What did the two boys on the computer do when he asked them if he could play with them? *(they started laughing at his bright yellow socks)*
4) Do you think it was right that all the other children were staring and pointing?
5) Have you ever felt that people were staring at you? *(Invite responses.)* How did you feel?
6) Why do you think the other children began to be friendlier when the other boy arrived? *(because they saw that he wasn't treating the little boy any differently just because he was wearing bright yellow socks)*

Getting the message – what can I do about it?
The little boy was treated unfairly because some children thought he looked different. Do you think it's fair to treat people differently because they look different? *(Invite responses.)* The way we look shouldn't matter. We are all special, we all have gifts – we are all unique. There are lots of people in the world who are treated badly or unfairly just because their skin is a different colour. Everybody in the world has the same rights, which means we should all be treated fairly. We can all remember this and treat people how we want to be treated.

Learning more
Today we have been thinking about respecting people and not discriminating against them. Discriminating means treating people badly and judging them for silly reasons. If you are not treated fairly, you should tell your teacher but we must all be responsible for treating others fairly too.

Non-interactive Follow-up

Summary
- The little boy was looking forward to his first day at school.
- He saw all the interesting things to learn about and play with when he went into the classroom.
- He asked two boys to play and they started laughing at his yellow socks.
- The other children began pointing and staring and the little boy felt uncomfortable.
- Another boy came in and asked him to play. He hadn't noticed the yellow socks.
- The other children felt uncomfortable about treating the little boy unfairly.
- Everybody is unique and special. Our colour or what we look like doesn't matter.
- Everyone should be treated equally and with respect. Always treat others how you want to be treated.

Reflection
The world is made up of people who are all different. It is all these differences that make our world such an interesting place. Everyone is special and unique. We all want to be liked and loved.

Prayer
Lord God,
Thank you for all the different people in the world and for all their gifts and the things that make each one of us special. Help us to always be kind to each other and forgive us for any times that we may not have been.
Amen.

2 POLLUTION SOLUTION

Objective
To raise children's awareness of the extent of pollution and to encourage them to reduce waste.

Links
Citizenship
2a: to research, discuss and debate topical issues, problems and events
2j: that resources can be allocated in different ways and that these economic choices affect individuals, communities and the sustainability of the environment

Props
- Plastic carrier bags with lots of goods that have waste packaging, e.g. plastic trays, plastic bags, plastic drink bottles, yoghurt pots, etc.
- Lunch with sandwiches in plastic bag or ready-made one, canned drink, sandwich container and re-usable drink container.
- Cleaning materials.
- Eco-Friendly cleaning materials.
- Selection of re-usable plastic bottles and containers.
- Bicycle, if possible!

Note: this assembly needs 2 teachers to act out the 'play'.

INTRODUCTION

Right, everyone stand up and take a few deep breaths! Can you feel your rib cage moving in and out? *(Demonstrate where rib cage is.)* Anyone know what's behind your ribcage? *(lungs)* That's right, your lungs! *(Tell children to sit down.)* Your lungs take in lots of air or oxygen. We need air to stay alive. But how clean is the air we breathe? A lot of the things that make our lives more comfy such as cars, electricity and heating, create bad gases which make the air dirty. That's called pollution. Pollution is waste – things that we don't need. The bad gases that go into the air are the gases which are waste from the things that we use – like coal fires, cars and heating. It's not just the air that gets dirty, though. All the things we throw away, which can't be used again, pollute the Earth. Can anyone think of things that we throw away? *(e.g. plastic bags, bottles and packages, etc)* W all need to be a lot more 'green' or, in other words, think about all the things we use every day and how we can cut down on our waste. Let's take a look at one person who doesn't really think about what he/she throws away or what he/she uses to help cut down on pollution.

Play: The not-so-green teacher

Teacher 1 *(bringing in lots of shopping bags with goods that are all heavily packaged in plastic, e.g. veg, plastic bottles of drink, yoghurts, cleaning items, etc)* Hello there. *(to children)* Look, I've been shopping. Got lots of bargains – lovely yoghurts, drinks, cakes *(adapt to whatever goods you've got)*.

Teacher 2 *(sternly)* I'm not very impressed.

Teacher 1 *(crossly)* What d'you mean?

Teacher 2 Don't you know anything? Look at all the packaging on these things. Don't you know that we're supposed to be cutting down on the amount of things we throw away? You just don't listen!

(Adapt this to say, for example, your head teacher had told you all to buy things with less waste – personalise it to the school.)

Teacher 1 *(looks upset)* Oh dear. Well, what can I do?

Teacher 2 You can take all this lot back for a start! All this waste just causes more pollution!

Teacher 1 *(crying)* But it took me ages, and my trolley kept going the wrong way, and...

Teacher 2 Don't be pathetic. Now listen – we'll take all this lot back and we'll get things that have hardly any packaging.

Teacher 1 *(sniffing)* Oh all right then. What about these, though? I thought we'd clean the staff room because you know what those messy teachers are like! *(produces all sorts of chemical cleaners)*

Teacher 2 *(rolling eyes)* Worse and worse! Full of chemicals and nasty, horrible things – they just cause pollution when you use them. Look, these are the kinds of cleaners you should use. *(Produces eco-friendly cleaning selection and points them out to children.)* They don't harm anything or anyone! Make sure you get them next time! *(Other teacher looks ashamed.)*

Teacher 1 Oh, alright then. But, before we go, I'm just going to have my lunch. *(Produces ready-made sandwich in packaging or in plastic bag, canned drink.)*

Teacher 2 Not again! You're not doing that again – tomorrow I want to see your sandwiches in this *(produce re-usable container)* and your drink in this *(produce re-usable container)*. No more plastic bags, packaging or cans, right?

Teacher 1 *(shaking head)* I'm not having a good day. Shall I go and get the car so we can go to the shop?

Teacher 2 You will not, I'm going on this *(produces bicycle [if possible] and rides out of the hall [if possible!])* and you're walking!
(Or, if no bicycle:) We're walking!

Teacher 1 *(runs after, clutching all the bags)* Wait for me!

Well, that teacher wasn't very 'green', was he? He certainly didn't know that to cut pollution we have to cut down on the amount of waste we throw away. But we know that, don't we? If we have less waste, that means we won't use our natural resources like trees and oil and coal so much. That means there'll be more to go round for everyone. If you see your teachers using things that make a lot of waste, make sure you tell them off!

INTERACTIVE FOLLOW-UP

Questions
1. What's behind your ribcage? *(lungs)*
2. What's another word for pollution? *(waste)*
3. What kinds of things pollute the air? *(cars, heating, coal fires)*
4. What things did the teacher do that weren't green? *(bought food and goods with lots of packaging; brought his lunch in lots of packaging; bought cleaners that had lots of chemicals; wanted to use the car instead of walking or biking)*
5. How could we cut down on our packed lunch waste? *(bring things in reusable containers)*
6. Why is walking better than using a car? *(because it doesn't use petrol and it's healthier)*

Getting the message – what can I do about it?
There are lots and lots of ways you, yes you, can help reduce pollution. You might think that what one person does isn't important, but it is! If we all did it, the difference would be amazing. A very famous person called Gandhi once said, 'You might think that what you do is unimportant, but it is VERY important that you do it.' In other words, you can make a difference!

Learning more
So how can I make a difference?

- Well, for a start, you can walk more and go in the car less. Persuade your mums and dads to walk or bike rather than drive. And you'll be super healthy!
- Go on a bus or train – they carry more people, so less energy is used and less pollution is caused.
- Turn off lights and any electrical things you're not using.
- Recycle all your rubbish that can be recycled.
- Use more reusable containers in your packed lunches.

Non-interactive Follow-up

Summary
- Your lungs are behind your ribcage and, when we breathe, our rib cages go in and out because our lungs expand and contract.
- Pollution is waste.
- Cars, heating and other forms of energy consumption pollute the air.
- The teacher brought goods with lots of packaging, cleaning materials full of chemicals, a packed lunch with lots of packaging and wanted to use the car instead of walking or biking.
- We can cut down on our packed lunch waste by using reusable containers.
- Walking and biking is much better because it doesn't cause pollution and it's healthy.

Reflection
Think of your home and the way that you travel, perhaps to school or at the weekends. Could you cut down on pollution in any way?

Prayer
Dear Lord,
We know that there is too much waste in the world. Help us to make a difference in our homes and at school. Help us to remember to try and recycle when we can, save energy when we can and to walk whenever we can.
Amen.

3 RECYCLING

Objectives
To learn [...] easy and important it is to make a difference to our e[...]

Links
PSHE/[...]
1c: to [...] information, looking for help, making responsible choice[...]
2a: to [...] problems and events

Pro[...]
2 waste paper bins [...] with supermarket carrier bags; four boxes (with optional labels indicating glass, paper, plastic and tin can recycling); a selection of 'rubbish', including 4 empty, rinsed jam jars, 4 newspapers, 4 empty, rinsed plastic milk containers, and 4 empty, rinsed tin cans. You will also need several volunteers – choose confident children who are good at listening to instructions: they will be required to pick up items of rubbish and put them into the correct bins. The bin belonging to the Browns should already have one of each type of rubbish in; the Sangs' bin should be empty, but their recycling boxes should contain one item of rubbish each. This adds to the bulk of the rubbish at the end of the story and makes the point more forcefully.

Handwritten note:
- Mr Brown – newspaper
- Mr Sang – " "
- Mrs Brown – jam jar
- Mrs Sang – " "
- Salif + Stephen – tins
- Eddah + Jessica – plastic

INTRODUCTION

This assembly is going to be a load of old rubbish! I don't mean it's not going to be much good – I mean that it's going to be about rubbish and what happens to it. We're going to have a look at two different families and see what they do with their rubbish.

Story
(Starting on right hand side of hall.) This is where the Browns live. They have a lovely big bin to put their rubbish in, to keep their house tidy. *(Show waste paper bin.)* I need four volunteers to be Mr and Mrs Brown and their children, Stephen and Jessica. Thank you. Come and stand here and I'll tell you what to do in a minute. *(Going over to left hand side of hall.)* This is where the Sang family live. They've got a nice big rubbish bin too, but they've also got some extra boxes here – we'll find out what they're for later. I need four people to be Mr and Mrs Sang and their children, Salif *(m)* and Eddah *(f)*. Lovely – you come and stand in your house here.

(Going back to the Browns' 'house' on the right, choosing a child and giving him a newspaper.) Now, Mr Brown here has just finished reading his newspaper, so *(motion child to put newspaper in the bin)* he puts it into his bin. He's a very tidy, chap, you see, and doesn't leave his rubbish lying about. Well done, Mr Brown!

(Return to left hand side, to the Sangs' 'house'.) Mr Sang over in his house has also just finished reading his newspaper, and wants to throw it away. But he doesn't put it in the bin - instead he puts it into this special box here. *(Motion child to put newspaper in the paper-recycling box.)* Thanks, Mr Sang.

Now, back at the Browns' house, Mrs Brown has just finished a jar of lovely strawberry jam and she's going to throw that away in her bin. *(Motion child to put jam jar in the bin.)* Fantastic. Oh look, here comes Mrs Sang, with her empty jam jar. Is she going to put that in the bin, I wonder? No – she puts it into the special box over here. *(Motion child to put jam jar in the glass-recycling box. Repeat these actions with fizzy drink cans and milk containers – the Browns' children put their rubbish into their bin and the Sangs' children put theirs into the relevant recycling boxes.)*

(To volunteers.) Well done to all of you. I hope that you're as tidy and helpful as that at home! You can sit down now.

INTERACTIVE FOLLOW-UP

Questions
1) Who can tell me what's in Mr and Mrs Brown's bin? *(Show each item from the bin as it's called out.)*
2) Now, what about Mr and Mrs Sang's bin? *(Show empty bin.)*
3) Where did they put their rubbish? *(Show recycling boxes.)*
4) Who knows why they put their rubbish into different boxes instead of putting it all into the same bin? *(To enable the rubbish to be recycled.)*

Getting the message
(Picking up the bin bag and its contents from the Browns' bin.) What do you think will happen to the rubbish when it's collected? I'll give you three choices, and I want you to give me a big 'thumbs up' *(illustrate)* for the right answers, and a big 'thumbs down' *(illustrate)* for the wrong answers.
- It gets made into something useful.
- It gets dumped on a huge rubbish dump and stays there.
- It gets burned.

Well, some of it does get put on a rubbish dump and some of it gets burned, so most of you got that right – well done. I need a bin man to come and take away the Browns' rubbish for me and put it on the rubbish dump here. *(Get volunteer and ask them to put the bag in the middle of the floor.)* Hands up who can think of problems that that might cause?
- Landfill sites get full and eventually we'll run out of space. Not all rubbish is nice and clean like this, the clean stuff is mixed with smelly rubbish, so they aren't nice to live near.
- Burning causes smoke and air pollution.

Learning more

Now let's have a look at the Sangs' rubbish. I'll need another bin man, please. *(Get volunteer.)* This box has the Sangs' glass jars and bottles in. It goes to a special factory where the glass is crushed and melted down, and then made into more glass jars and bottles. *(Ask bin man to take the box and put it to one side. Bin man picks up each subsequent box, holds it up for children to see and then puts it to one side.)* Now for Mr Sang's newspaper: the paper goes to a factory where it gets all mushed up and the old paper is used to make new paper. The plastic is also taken away to a factory, where it is turned into new plastic containers, and the tin cans are made into new cans.

So, all of the things that the Browns threw away, and ended up on a huge great smelly rubbish heap, could have been turned into new and useful things, like the Sangs' rubbish was. Who knows what word we use for using old rubbish to make new, useful things? *(recycling)*

We've only seen what can happen to one single bag of rubbish, and perhaps one or two jam jars don't seem very important. Just think, though:
- What would happen if NOBODY recycled their rubbish? *(Landfill sites would grow and grow and we'd run out of space for the rubbish.)*
- What would happen if EVERYBODY recycled their rubbish? *(Landfill sites would grow much more slowly.)*

NON-INTERACTIVE FOLLOW-UP

Summary
- The Browns and the Sangs are both tidy families who throw their rubbish away carefully.
- The Browns throw everything into one rubbish bin.
- Their rubbish gets collected by the bin men and gets burned or thrown on a landfill site.
- The Sangs separate out their rubbish.
- Each type of rubbish goes to a recycling plant to be made into new and useful products.

Reflection
It's quite easy to separate out our rubbish and get it recycled: in some parts of the country you need to take your old paper, glass, plastics and metal cans to a recycling centre, but in many places you can get it collected from your home. By recycling our rubbish, we can all help to make our world a better, cleaner place. Think carefully next time you throw something away: could that thing be recycled and turned into something useful, or will it end up being wasted and taking up valuable space on a rubbish tip?

Prayer
Dear Lord,
Thank you for the wonderful world you have given us to live in. We're sorry that we don't always take care of it as we should. Please help us to try to take care of it a bit better by recycling our rubbish, instead of being lazy and just throwing it all away.
Amen.

4 A Local Citizen is a Global Citizen

Objective
For children to learn about the benefits of contributing to their local community.

Links
Citizenship
1a: to talk and write about their opinions, and explain their views on issues that affect themselves and society
5a: take responsibility
5d: make real choices and decisions

Props
Globe or map of the world to project.

Introduction

Have you ever been to a jumble sale or fete? *(Invite responses.)* There are all sorts of things you can go to, aren't there? Have you ever wondered, though, who organises those sorts of things? Today we're going to hear a story about a little girl who did organise something and what happened when she did!

Story: The concert
Jessica lived in a small village in the country. There was a shop and post office, a village hall, a telephone box, two churches and lots of farms and houses dotted around. There weren't really any houses which were right next door to each other, but everyone knew each other anyway. There used to be a school in the village several years ago but now that was closed and the children had to go to school in a village about five miles away. Jessica and the other children travelled there every day on the school bus. Lots of things happened in the village hall, and there was a nice big green next to it where people had picnics and things when there was a jumble sale or at the Annual Village Show, but there wasn't really anywhere that Jessica and her friends could go to play.

It would have been great to have somewhere on the green with a slide and swings and a climbing frame – maybe even a roundabout. The nearest play park was about 10 miles away and Jessica's mum didn't take her very often at all, partly because she was very busy and partly because it was in the opposite direction to the way they usually went. Jessica thought about this a lot but she had no idea how one could be built. She supposed it would cost a lot of money and all she had was 20 pence in her money box, so that wouldn't go very far.

One day, when she and her mum and dad were driving past another village hall a few miles from her home, Jessica saw a sign saying 'Coffee morning' and 'Help raise money to improve our Hall'. She suddenly thought – why don't I try and raise money for a play park! She got very excited and said to her mum and dad, 'I'm going to try and raise some money for a play park!'

Her mum and dad said, 'That's a great idea – what are you going to do?'

Jessica opened her mouth and then realised she didn't know what she was going to do! You wouldn't be able to raise much by selling a few measly coffees! 'I don't know,' she said a bit despondently. Over the next few days, Jessica thought and thought but couldn't really think of anything unusual to do. Until she and her friends were messing about playing their instruments and singing – and then it came to her!

'We'll put on a concert!' she shouted to her friends, very excitedly. 'I'll ask Mr Watson from the Post Office to play the piano for us if we need it (he's really good) and we can all do something! What do you think?' All her friends agreed – there were all sorts of things they could do – Millie did Irish Dancing; Robert and James would do a judo demonstration; Matthew played the trombone; Jessica would play the flute; Rosie would do some ballet – the list started to get longer and longer. All the children wanted to do something and the grown-ups too! Even Mrs Walsh (who was sometimes a bit crabby) said that she would make some cookies and provide drinks in the interval.

They started to plan immediately – Mr Watson said of course he'd play and they all began to make posters, design tickets and write programmes – everything they would need to make the concert a success. Then Jessica and Rosie did the most important sign of all to put outside the hall for people to see when they went past. It said, 'PLEASE COME TO OUR CONCERT AND HELP US RAISE MONEY FOR OUTSIDE PLAY EQUIPMENT'.

When the day of the concert arrived, the village hall was full and the whole thing was a great success. At the end of the evening, Mr Townsend, who was chairman of the Village Hall Committee, told everyone that the concert had raised £300. Everyone clapped and cheered. Then he said, 'We've looked at the cost of putting a slide, swings, climbing frame and a roundabout on the green of the Village Hall. It would cost £1,000. So we haven't got enough.' Jessica was very upset and could feel her eyes starting to fill up. But, then, Mr Townsend said, 'Jessica will you come here please?' Jessica went to the front of the hall, a bit scared. 'If this little girl hadn't thought of raising money for some play equipment, the Village Hall Committee would never have thought of it. We think it's a marvellous idea and we are going to make up the rest of the money from Village Hall Funds. So that means the equipment will be here in less than a month! Well done Jessica, you've really helped the village. Lots of children will be able to use the equipment, not just now but in the future as well. We're all very proud of you.' Jessica couldn't believe it - and everyone clapped and cheered again.

INTERACTIVE FOLLOW-UP

Questions

1. Where did Jessica live? *(in a small village)*
2. Where did she and her friends go to school? *(in another village a few miles away)*
3. What did Jessica think would be a good thing to have on the green next to the village hall? *(some play park equipment – swings, slide, climbing frame, roundabout)*
4. Where was the nearest play park to Jessica? *(about 10 miles away)*
5. What made Jessica think of raising some money to buy some play park equipment? *(She saw a sign outside another village hall where they were having a coffee morning to raise money to improve their village hall.)*
6. What did Jessica and her friends decide to do to raise some money? *(hold a concert)*
7. Can you remember how much they raised? *(£300)*
8. Was it enough to buy play park equipment? *(No, they needed £1,000.)*
9. What happened at the end of the concert? *(Mr Townsend said that the Village Hall Committee would make up the rest of the money so that they could buy the play equipment.)*
10. What did Mr Townsend say to Jessica? *(that she had really helped the village)*
11. Why do you think Jessica had really helped the village? *(because the play equipment could be used by lots of families, not just now but in the future as well)*

Getting the message – what can I do about it?

We are all citizens! Can anyone tell me what a citizen is? *(someone who lives in a city, town or village)* Jessica was a citizen in her village; she belonged there just like all the other people who lived in her village. She also wanted to make life better, not just for herself, but for the other children in her village as well. To do that, she had to make an effort and get other people involved in her idea. Sometimes that can be hard, but Jessica managed it and made the grown-ups get involved as well! Jessica was well and truly part of her community. We can all be involved like Jessica if we notice something that might improve life for others as well as for ourselves.

Learning more

We're all citizens of the city, town or village where we live – but we're also citizens of the world too! *(Project map or show globe at this point. Discuss with children where the UK is and any other countries the children know about.)* I'm sure you've all seen charity shops, but do you know where they get all the things from that they sell? *(Invite responses.)* That's right – from you and me! If you clear out your clothes and toys regularly and take them to the charity shops to sell, then you're helping people straight away. The shops sell stuff to make money to give to the people who need it! Can anyone think of any charity shops you might be able to take your stuff to? *(Invite responses.)* Well done, we all know loads of places we can take things to – and, while you're at it, make sure you ask the rest of your family to do the same!

Being a citizen of where you live and also of the world is all about how you choose to live your life. Do you think it's wrong that some people don't have as much money or food as others? Hands up. *(Pause.)* Are you careful about switching things off at home and at school so that you don't use up energy resources? Hands up. *(Pause.)* Do you care whether the things you and your family buy might make life better or worse for people? Hands up. *(Pause.)* That's great – what a lot of hands! I know that you'll make sure that you continue to care about things as you grow up so that you'll all be the best global and local citizens ever!

Non-interactive Follow-up

Summary
- Jessica lived in a small village.
- She wished there was a place with outdoor play equipment where she and her friends could play in the village.
- She was inspired to raise money when she saw another village holding a coffee morning to improve their hall.
- At first she couldn't think what to do, then she and her friends decided to put on a concert.
- They raised £300 but the play equipment cost £1,000.
- The Village Hall Committee were so pleased with Jessica's idea that they decided to give the rest of the money from village hall funds to buy the play equipment.
- Jessica helped her local community to provide something that would improve life for children for the future.

Reflection
Jessica decided to get involved and do something and that is what being a citizen is about – action! If you wait for someone else to do something, it probably won't happen. So if you think you want to try and improve your life, your community's and that of other people in the world who are not as lucky as us – then do something. Make a start by asking your mums and dads to buy things from charity shops – even if it's just cards; or take any stuff that can be sold to make money. You might do that already, in which case – great. If you don't, maybe you could start to think about it with your family. We are all part of our local community and environment. We use schools, swimming pools, shops, libraries, parks and lots of other things. There are always things we can do to help protect and improve the environment – even if it's just picking up litter.

Prayer
Lord God,
Help us to lead lives which are worthwhile and help us to help others when we can.
Amen.

5 Fairtrade

Objective
To raise children's awareness of Fairtrade and for them to begin to understand the role of pressure and voluntary groups in campaigns to improve human rights.

Links
Religious Education
2d: reflect on ideas of right and wrong and their own and others' responses to them
3m: beliefs in action in the world: how religions and beliefs respond to global issues of human rights, fairness, social justice and the importance of the environment

Citizenship
2h: to recognise the role of voluntary, community and pressure groups
5d: make real choices and decisions

Props
Globe or world map/map of Windward Islands to project.
A bunch of Fairtrade bananas in pack and an ordinary bunch of bananas, plus one extra.
An assortment of 6 straw hats *(not essential)* and one naval officer-type cap *(if possible)*.
A spade, blue plastic, blunt knife, cardboard box.
Toy driving wheel or toy truck, toy ship.
Tesco bag.
Fairtrade logo to show or project.
Pictures of green bananas being harvested to project (optional).
Other Fairtrade goods (optional).

INTRODUCTION

(Produce a banana and show it.) Who likes bananas? Lots of you, that's good. I do too. Lots of people in the UK do too – each year we all eat at least 20 bunches of bananas each! Where do you think bananas come from? *(Invite responses and make comments according to suggestions.)* They actually come from a long way away from here. A lot come from a group of Caribbean islands called the Windward Islands. *(Show globe or project world map and islands at this point – show children where the UK is as well, or ask someone to point it out, so that they can begin to have an understanding of how far away places are.)* Most of us buy our bananas at the supermarket or you might buy some from a greengrocer. Wherever your mums and dads buy them from, a lot has happened to a banana before it finally gets into our tummies! Let's find out.

The banana story

Can I have some volunteers please. *(Choose 10 children. Put straw hats on 6, a naval cap on one and give the last three a Tesco carrier bag, a bunch of Fairtrade bananas and a bunch of ordinary bananas. The 6 straw hat children should stand in a line, then the naval cap child, then the Tesco carrier bag and lastly the two banana bunches. Also, give the first child a spade, the second the blue plastic, the blunt knife to the third, the box to the fourth, the driving wheel to the fifth and the naval cap child should have the toy boat or ship. Explain to the children that you are going to describe how the bananas are grown, when you stand behind each of them, they should mime what you say. Move behind the first child.)*

Well, our journey starts here, so:

1. First of all, the land has to be cleared and a lot of digging has to be done. The banana plants are put in the ground and they begin to grow. *(Move to next child.)*
2. When the bananas are small, they are wrapped in blue plastic – that stops them from getting damaged. It also protects them against the nasty pesticides and chemicals. *(Move to next child.)*
3. After nine months, the bananas are cut off the plant or harvested. Does anyone know what colour the bananas are when they're picked? *(green)* The bunches that are picked are much bigger than the ones we buy in the shops – the clusters are called 'hands' and they have about 10 to 20 bananas in them. They are also called 'fingers' *(project pictures at this point if using, then move to next child)*.
4. After that, they are washed and labelled and put into boxes so that they don't get bruised. What does a banana look like if it's bruised? *(The skin goes black and it's brown and squashy inside. Move to next child.)*
5. Then they are driven from the farm to a warehouse in a truck. *(Move to next child.)*
6. This is taking a long time, isn't it? Well, after they're unloaded at the warehouse, they are all checked and inspected. If any are bruised or damaged, they have to be sold locally at a very low price. *(Move to next child.)*
7. Let's move on to the captain. Captain X takes them from the Windward Isles in his big ship *(they have to be put in a cool place so that they don't go yellow, otherwise they'll go off before they get to the shops)*. It takes 6 days for them to get to the UK and then they're taken to a special place where they're ripened and then finally... *(move to next child)*
8. They get to the shops and we buy them! *(Child holds up Tesco carrier bag – applause!)*

Now we've got two bunches of bananas here *(ask children to hold them up)*. Can anybody see any difference in them? *(Invite responses and then hold the Fairtrade bunch up.)* What can you see on this bunch that isn't on this bunch? That's right; it's got the Fairtrade logo on it. *(Project or show the Fairtrade logo at this point.)* Who can tell me what Fairtrade means? *(Invite responses and respond accordingly, then expand.)* If you buy something that is Fairtrade, with this logo, it means that the farmers who planted and grew the bananas here *(move back to first children)* will get a fair price for the bananas they have sold for us to eat. They will have enough money to eat, send their children to school and pay for medicines, if necessary. They also get a bit extra which helps their community or where they live to perhaps have a hospital built or more nurses and doctors to work there.

Now, if we buy these bananas *(ask child to hold other bunch up)*, it means that the farmers probably haven't got a fair price for their bananas and they'll have had to use lots of horrible chemicals, plus they won't have enough money to eat or send their children to school or buy medicine.

Which bananas do you think we should buy? *(Invite responses.)* The Fairtrade ones? I think so too. If we can help people to live a better life, then that's what we should do.

INTERACTIVE FOLLOW-UP

Questions
1) Where do a lot of bananas come from? *(Windward Islands)*
2) What has to be done before bananas can be planted? *(The land has to be cleared.)*
3) What happens next? *(They're wrapped in blue plastic.)*
4) Why are they wrapped in blue plastic? *(To protect them from being bruised and to protect them from chemicals and pesticides.)*
5) How long is it before they're harvested? *(nine months)*
6) What colour are they when they're picked and what are the clusters called? *(green, hands or fingers)*
7) What happens after they've been washed and inspected, put into boxes and driven to the warehouse? *(They are sent by ship to the UK.)*
8) What happens to the ones that are bruised or damaged? *(They're sold at a much lower price locally.)*
9) What kind of bananas should we buy if possible? *(Fairtrade)*
10) Why? *(because the farmers get a fair price and they can afford to eat, send their children to school and buy medicine)*

Getting the message – what can I do about it?
Now you know the life story of a banana, next time you go shopping look out for the Fairtrade logo on the packs. They do cost a little bit extra, but if you persuade your mums and dads to buy them, you'll know that the people who grew them are getting a fair deal. Organisations like Oxfam and The Fairtrade Foundation have been trying to persuade supermarkets to stock Fairtrade bananas for a long time. If people don't buy them, they might stop stocking them! That would be terrible. If you notice that the shop where you buy your bananas doesn't have Fairtrade ones, ask them to get them! We shoppers have a lot of power – it's us that are spending the money!

Learning more
Did you know that it's not just Fairtrade bananas that you can buy? Does anyone know what other things you can buy that are Fairtrade? *(tea, coffee, chocolate, biscuits, fruit juice)* Look out for the Fairtrade logo when you're in the supermarket with your mums and dads and see if you can spot any others. If you want to find out more about Fairtrade, look on their website (www.fairtrade.org.uk), which gives lots of information.

NON-INTERACTIVE FOLLOW-UP

Summary
- Lots of bananas come from the Windward Isles.
- The land has to be cleared, holes dug and banana plants planted.
- The bananas are wrapped in blue plastic to prevent them from being bruised and to protect them from pesticides.
- The bananas are harvested after nine months. They grow in clusters called hands or fingers.
- They are washed, put into boxes and taken to a warehouse.
- Any bruised or damaged bananas are sold at a much lower price.
- They are shipped to the UK and then taken to the supermarkets.
- Oxfam and Fairtrade have successfully managed to get supermarkets to stock Fairtrade bananas after a long battle.
- If you buy Fairtrade, you know that the growers are receiving a decent wage for their families to live on.
- Goods other than bananas can be bought fairly traded.

Reflection
When you help your mums and dads do their shopping, tell them what you have learnt about Fairtrade and discuss with them about perhaps buying some things that have the Fairtrade logo. Everybody has the right to earn enough to eat and feed their families – if we can help make that happen, then we should!

Prayer
Lord God,

Thank you for organisations such as Oxfam and the Fairtrade Foundation, which are helping poor people to earn more and to have proper working conditions. Help us to remember that we too can help when we're shopping by looking for the Fairtrade logo and buying as many of those products as we can.

Amen.

6 Children's Rights

Objective
For children to understand that we all have the right to be treated fairly and to begin to understand the concept of a right.

Links
Citizenship
2c: to realise the consequences of anti-social and aggressive behaviours, such as bullying and racism.

Props
None.

Introduction

Have you ever gone somewhere new, like a club or maybe a new school? *(Invite responses.)* It's hard, isn't it? You have to get used to all the routines, the people and the different times that things happen. Maybe you've moved house and you don't really know anyone yet. This is a story about someone who started a new school and didn't really like it at first.

Story: The new school
Akashi was really looking forward to starting her new school, although she was a bit nervous. Her mum took her to her classroom and she met her teacher, who seemed really nice, and he showed her where her tray would be and where to put her coat and bag and things. It was OK during the morning, except she noticed that there were a few girls looking and pointing, but she concentrated on her numeracy work and reading and, before she knew it, it was playtime. Akashi got her snack and went into the playground. There were so many children!

Feeling a bit nervous, she went and stood by the wall and watched. Just as she was going to put a crisp in her mouth, two girls went past and grabbed the packet from her! 'Hey,' she shouted, 'give that back!' The two girls stopped and looked at Akashi.

'No,' one of them said, and then she added, 'Fat-face!' and ran off. Akashi was shocked and thought she was going to cry. But she took a deep breath and walked off in the opposite direction. But the girls came running up behind her again and then walked beside her, saying things like, 'We don't like you. You can't play with us.' Akashi kept walking, she had to get away from them. She kept her head down and longed for playtime to be over. Just then the whistle went and they all went back into the classroom.

When Akashi was sitting at her place, she realised that the two girls were in her class! 'Oh no,' thought Akashi and tried not to look at them. She learnt that their names were Sophie and Makayla. She was dreading lunchtime play.

When it arrived, Akashi went to the Adventure Playground, hoping to avoid them but they suddenly appeared, saying, 'Why have you come here? Go back to your new school.' Akashi tried to get away from them but they followed her and called her more names.

Just when she thought she really was going to cry, she heard another voice, but this time it was kind. 'Get lost you two. How would you feel if you were being followed like that.' Akashi looked up and saw a kind face and brown eyes. 'Hello,' the face said, 'I'm Dominic. Do you want to come and play with us?'

Akashi looked over and saw a group of about five children who were about to play a game. 'Yes, please,' said Akashi and followed Dominic to where the other children were. The next playtime was great!

INTERACTIVE FOLLOW-UP

Questions
- Who are the children in the story? *(Akashi, Sophie, Makayla and Dominic)*
- How was Akashi treated in the story? *(bullied)*
- Was this fair? *(no)*
- Is it hurtful for children to behave like that? How did Akashi feel? How would you feel? *(Invite responses and discuss.)*
- Why do you think the two girls, Makayla and Sophie, might have behaved like that? *(Invite responses.)*
- Have you ever been treated unfairly by anyone? *(Invite responses.)*

Getting the message – what can I do about it?
Akashi was treated unfairly in the story, wasn't she? Sometimes everybody can be unpleasant but, if somebody is in a situation where they don't know anyone and everything is new, it is particularly unfair. It was hard for Akashi to say anything but, fortunately, Dominic helped her and stopped the bullies. If you're ever in a situation where people are encouraging you to be nasty, turn away and refuse to join in. That can be hard if lots of people are trying to make you, but you should always do what you know is the right thing to do. If you do, it will mean you're a much stronger and braver person than the bullies.

Learning more
Everybody has the right to be treated fairly because we are all equally important. It is important to remember to always treat other people how you want to be treated.

Non-interactive Follow-up

Summary
- The main children in the story are Akashi, Sophie, Makayla and Dominic.
- Akashi was new to the school.
- Sophie and Makayla bullied her at playtime and called her names.
- Akashi was scared and dreaded playtimes.
- Dominic told the bullies to go away and asked Akashi to play with him and his friends.
- Everyone has the right to be treated fairly.
- We are all equally important.
- Treat others how you want to be treated.

Reflection
It is always upsetting when people are nasty. Everyone, young and old, has the right to be treated fairly and with respect. If we treat others well, we can expect to be treated well in return.

Prayer
Lord God,
Thank you that you have made so many different people in the world. Please forgive us if we have ever been nasty and help us not to be in the future. Help us all to treat each other with equal importance and with equal respect.
Amen.

7 Hunger

Objective
For children to be aware that not all countries have enough food for their population and that food provision in the world is not equal.

Links
Citizenship
2j: that resources can be allocated in different ways and that these economic choices affect individuals, communities and the sustainability of the environment

Props
A supply of biscuits, sliced fruit, sweets or some other appropriate food that can be divided between four children. *(Make sure it's something that can be clearly divided unevenly - e.g. Rebecca has 4 pieces, etc.)*

Note: If using biscuits or any other type of processed food, ensure that any volunteers do not have any allergies.

A globe.

Introduction

What's your favourite breakfast? *(Invite responses.)* Mine's porridge! *(Insert whatever is your favourite!)* Breakfast is the best meal of the day – and the most important - because it gives you energy to work and play all morning. We're very lucky, aren't we, because we have such a huge choice of food to eat. Do you think everybody has that choice? Let's investigate.

Does everyone get their fair share?
Can I have some volunteers please? *(Choose four older children and children who are unlikely to be upset at receiving less food!)* Now, these lucky children are going to get something extra to eat this morning! *(Pick up globe.)*

Let's look at this globe – can anyone tell me what this globe is supposed to be? That's right, it's the Earth. We're going to imagine that the world is divided into four equal parts or, in other words, parts that are the same size. I'm going to give some food out now – W is going to have 6 biscuits *(or whatever food you are using)*, X is going to have 3 biscuits, Y can have 1 biscuit and Z, well let me see, I think I've got a few crumbs left in the packet – yes! Here Z can have these crumbs. *(Look at the school.)* Now, that's fair, isn't it? *(Be prepared for choruses of no!)* Isn't it? *(Carry this on for a little bit so that children are outraged.)*

Of course, you're right. It's not fair at all, why should W get the most and Z get nothing? What do you think I should do? *(Invite responses. Ask X, Y and Z what they feel like; do they feel angry? What would they like to do? Allow the children to offer suggestions and solutions.)* We've all decided that these biscuits were not shared out fairly. So let's give everyone an equal share! *(Share food out equally.)*

But did you know that all the food in the world is shared out between people in exactly the way I did it first of all? In other words, one part of the world gets loads - that's us and other countries like America and the rest of Europe - does anyone know any other countries in Europe? *(Elicit other countries if possible and then name the rest, showing children on the globe. Explain to the children that those countries are known as 'The West'.)* One part of the world gets quite a lot less, another gets a lot less than that and the last part of the world gets hardly anything at all. Who thinks that's fair? You're right. It's not fair at all. Why do you think some people don't have enough to eat? *(Because they are poor, they can't grow food because of the weather or not enough land.)* There is enough food in the world for everyone to eat – the problem is not everyone can get it. It is the poor people who go hungry. They either do not own enough land to grow their own food or they do not have enough money to buy food when they can't grow it.

INTERACTIVE FOLLOW-UP

Questions
1) Who can tell me why it's important to have breakfast? *(because it gives you energy through the morning to work and play)*
2) Can you remember what we call all the countries who are very fortunate and have enough food to eat every day? *(the West)*
3) Why is it that some people don't have enough food? *(They are poor; they don't have enough land to grow food.)*

Getting the message – what can I do about it?
Can I have seven children out here please? *(Choose 7 children, ask 6 to stand to one side and 1 to stand on the other.)* Let's imagine that these children represent all the children in the world. For every seven children in the world, 6 will have enough food to eat *(indicate the 6)* and one child won't *(stand with the one child)*. Can I have another 7 volunteers please? *(Choose 7 more children, stand 6 with the other 6 children and 1 to stand with the other child on his/her own.)* So, now I've got 14 children at the front – 12 will have enough to eat, 2 won't, and so it goes on. As the numbers get bigger, there will be lots and lots of children and adults who don't have any or enough food.

So, do you think anyone is doing anything to help the people who don't have enough to eat? *(Invite responses; you might elicit charity organisations.)* There are organisations called charities which work very hard to help. You've probably heard of charities like Children in Need or Oxfam or Comic Relief – they work very hard to try and teach people about farming and to get food to them – people like you and me from rich countries give money to help them do this. But there are other things we can do, besides give money. If you have a good look in your bedroom, I bet you've got loads of things you don't play with any more or clothes that you've grown out of. If you gather them altogether and take them to a local charity shop, they can sell them to make money to send to the poorer countries to help them buy food. Ask your mums and dads! If your school supports a charity each year, ask if they can choose a charity that helps people who are hungry.

Learning more

In many poorer countries, the best land is used for growing crops to sell to richer countries, so that means the worst land, or land that isn't good enough to grow anything, is left for local people or, in other words, the people that live in the country. Very often it's not possible to grow food on the worst land, but there will still be plenty of food in the country – it is sold to other countries.

NON-INTERACTIVE FOLLOW-UP

Summary
- Breakfast is the most important meal of the day because it gives us energy to work and play in the morning.
- Not everyone in the world has the huge amount of choice in food that we have.
- Food is unequally shared out in the world; there is enough food for everyone.
- Poor people are the ones that go hungry. They don't have enough money to buy any food; they don't own enough land to grow things to feed themselves; the land might be poor so crops can't be grown anyway; or the weather affects the crops (drought or floods).
- We can help by taking any unwanted toys, clothes or books to our local charity shop for them to sell. We can also ask our school to support a charity that helps feed the poor.

Reflection

There is more than enough food in the world to feed everyone. Sometimes, if we don't like something that we are given to eat, we should remember the people in the world who have hardly anything to eat.

Prayer

Lord God,
Thank you that you have provided enough food in the world for everyone to eat. We pray that you will help the richer countries to divide the food more fairly so that everyone has enough. Remind us to help the poor people of the world by clearing out things we don't need and giving anything we can afford to charities that help feed the hungry.
Amen.

8 Peace and Conflict

Objective
For children to recognise some of the causes of conflict and to encourage them to think about resolving issues and learning from mistakes.

Links
Citizenship
4a: that their actions affect themselves and others, to care about other people's feelings and to try to see things from their points of view

Props
Soft ball.
Large book (any kind of topic book, but one that is big enough to share with three children).
Packet of sweets.

Introduction

Have you ever been in the playground and wanted to join in a game and someone told you that you couldn't? Or has anyone ever been reading a book that looked really interesting in class reading-session and they wouldn't let you share it? It's not very nice being left out, is it? Let's look at how those kinds of situations might make you feel.

Dramas: Can I join in?
Can I have three volunteers please? *(Choose three children.)* Now, we're going to look at three different situations. The first one is in the playground. *(Give two of the children the soft ball and ask the other child to stand at the other side of the hall, explain to the child on his/her own that he/she should walk over to the two playing and ask to join in, tell the children who are playing to refuse to let the other child join them – encourage children to improvise - e.g. the other child can ask why he/she isn't being allowed to join in and answers can be thought of.)*

That wasn't very nice, was it? Who thinks they were a bit mean? What should they have done? *(Invite responses, then address the child who was left out.)* How did you feel about them not letting you play with them? *(Allow child the opportunity to respond.)* How do you think you would have felt? *(Address school and invite responses.)*

Now let's look at a different situation, this time we're in the classroom. *(Give 2 of the children the topic book. Change the children round, so that the child who was left out before is now sharing the book with one of the others and a different child is left out – again ask the children to improvise with asking to join in and responses.)*

Well, I hope none of you ever do that! All he/she wanted was to have a look at the book! *(Address both child and school again and invite responses.)* Let's try one more. *(Ensure that the child who is left out this time is the one that hasn't been in the previous scenarios and give one of the other two a packet of sweets; this time the children with the sweets refuse to share.)*

Again, not very nice! *(Repeat questioning as before.)*

INTERACTIVE FOLLOW-UP

Questions
1) Who's ever left someone out of something? *(Invite responses.)*
2) That's very honest *(depending on your replies!)*. If you're ever tempted to do that, what do you think you should try and remember? *(How would you feel if it was you being left out?)*
3) What should you do rather than fight? *(Tell a teacher or a friend.)*
4) If you do make a mistake, what's the best thing to do? *(Learn from it and not do it again.)*

Getting the message
Who was in the wrong in all these situations? *(The children who wouldn't share.)* Now each of these children was the child who was left out in the different situations, and they all felt upset and confused *(include any other words children have used)* when they were told they couldn't join in or have any sweets. Now, supposing I hadn't been around when, for example, X asked Y to join the ball game. What might have happened? *(fighting)* What do you think is a better thing to do rather than fight? *(Invite responses – elicit tell teacher or peer mediator.)* That's right, if you find yourself in that situation, tell someone else – either a friend who can help you join in or a teacher. Everyone makes mistakes sometimes, especially when we're really enjoying ourselves and we think someone else might spoil our fun. But it's never kind to leave anyone out of a game – try and think how you would feel if it was you asking to join in! That way, we learn from our mistakes and do the right thing in future.

Learning more
If you find yourself in trouble, the best way is to ask for help and apologise if you've done anything wrong. It takes courage to say you're sorry and it also helps you to see things from someone else's point of view. It shows that you respect a person, which is very important.

Non-interactive Follow-up

Summary
- It is important not to make people feel left out when we are playing or sharing things, like sweets.
- Always ask a teacher or someone you trust if you find yourself in a situation where you are starting to get cross and upset.
- Apologise if you have done anything wrong.
- If you make a mistake, learn from it and try not to do it again.

Reflection
When people are being unkind, it's sometimes hard to understand. But we should always treat people how we want to be treated – that means respectfully and with kindness.

Prayer
Lord God,
Help us always to be kind to people and to treat them with respect, as we wish to be treated. If we do make a mistake, give us the courage to apologise and to learn from it.
Amen.

9 Be Cool, Save our Fuel!
Energy Resources

Objective
To raise children's awareness of the need to conserve energy resources and of the need to take action to help slow down global warming.

Links
Citizenship
1a: to talk about their opinions and explain views on issues that affect themselves and society
1j: that resources can be allocated in different ways and that these economic choices affect individuals, communities and the sustainability of the environment

Props
None.

INTRODUCTION

Hands up if you're going to work hard today! Hands up if you're going to play hard today! What do we need to have to do both those things? *(energy)* Hands up if you can tell me what 'energy' is? *(Energy is the ability to do work.)* Hands up if you've got lots of energy! What do we have to have to give us energy? *(food)* When we eat food, our bodies store the energy until we need it for working and playing, then we need to have some more food to get some more energy and so it goes on! Today we're going to talk about energy and what makes it. It's a very important part of our lives.

It's very important to eat properly so that our bodies have enough energy for all the things we have to do. Is it just people who work? *(Elicit machines, cars, etc.)* No, it isn't. We need energy to make 'things' work like computers, cars – can you think of anything else that needs 'energy' to make it work? *(Invite responses.)* That's right, we use energy for all sorts of things – electricity, cars, heating and making things like toys and clothes. But do all these things eat food to give them energy? No, of course they don't. What gives them energy, then? *(Invite responses.)* They use fuels, like oil, coal and gas, which are all 'fossil' fuels because they took a long time to form in the earth. Once they are all used, it will take millions of years for them to return or 'renew'. So we need to make sure that we save energy for making things work as much as we can. Here's a story about a little boy who didn't realise that, but soon did after someone paid him a visit!

Story: Be cool, save our fuel!

Lewis lived with his mum, dad and sister, Ruth, in a big house in the countryside. Lewis was very lucky because he had lots of toys and his very own room, in which he had a computer, a television and lots of different kinds of lights – a spotlight for when he was doing his homework at his desk; a main light for when he needed to see things clearly in his room (especially when he was looking for his socks and his hamster – which was most nights); a bedside light for reading in bed and a really cool globe night-light which he didn't turn off at night because he liked looking at the colours.

Lewis very often went to bed without shutting down his computer and leaving his television with the red standby light on. He didn't see the point of shutting them down because he was going to use them the next day anyway! Actually, it wasn't just Lewis who left things on – his mum, dad and sister did too! That's probably why he did. Anyway, one night he'd been looking for Snooky, his hamster, as usual, and all the lights were on as well as his computer and television, when he heard a voice say to him – 'You really should turn those off you know.'

Lewis scrambled out from underneath the bed and saw a boy about the same size as him wearing a sort of superhero type costume with a cloak as well. The costume was bright green and it had 'SNOOKY SAYS BE COOL, SAVE OUR FUEL' written on it in bright yellow. Lewis stared at him, open-mouthed. 'Who are you?' he managed to say.

'Let's just say I help people to save our planet,' said the boy. 'You can call me Snooky,' he added.

'That's my hamster's name,' said Lewis.

'That's right,' said Snooky.

'He's the one that let me know about you leaving everything on. He wants to have a snooze in peace so that you don't find him every night!' Lewis was still staring open-mouthed. 'Do you know,' said Snooky, 'how much fuel you and your family are wasting? It's not going to last forever you know.' Snooky wandered over to Lewis' computer and television. 'You should turn these off when you're not using them and all the lights when you go out of your room. If you do that, you'll help to save our fuel for people in the future. Tell your mum, dad and sister too – they're just as bad!'

Lewis thought. 'You mean all the time I'm leaving things on, I'm using fuel that I don't need? So I'm wasting it?'

'That's right,' said Snooky.

'That's terrible,' said Lewis. 'I didn't realise. I'll tell Mum, Dad and Ruth that we mustn't waste so much fuel in the future.'

'Well done,' said Snooky. 'And while you're at it, think about walking to school – you lot use loads of petrol! Think how much healthier you'll be. And you'll be helping to save fuel for people in the future.'

'You're right,' said Lewis, turning off his computer and monitor. He turned round to say something else to Snooky but couldn't see him, all he could see was his hamster, who had somehow got tangled up in his green socks and was looking up at him as if to say, 'Get me out of these!' Lewis blinked – had he imagined that conversation? Had he imagined Snooky? He didn't know but he did know that in future he would turn things off!

Lewis understood at last that it was very wasteful of him to leave everything on! We use a lot of energy in our homes – heating to keep us warm but also for water to give us baths and showers; cooking; fridges; washing machines; dishwashers – the list is endless! We also use energy to get ourselves to different places – cars, buses, aeroplanes! They all use fossil fuels – in other words, fuel that can't be renewed. Everyone has got to try and save energy for people in the future. We can't stop using energy but we can try to use less.

INTERACTIVE FOLLOW-UP

Questions
1. What is energy? *(the ability to work)*
2. What gives us energy? *(food)*
3. What other things do we use that need energy? *(heating, televisions, computers, dishwashers, washing machines, cookers, cars, buses, aeroplanes, etc)*
4. What kind of fuels are oil, coal and gas? *(fossil fuels)*
5. What does 'fossil' fuels mean? *(It means it took millions of years for them to be made from fossils in the earth.)*
6. Can they be renewed? *(No, because it would take too long.)*
7. Why was Lewis lucky? *(He had lots of toys and electrical things.)*
8. Who did he look for under the bed? *(Snooky, his hamster)*
9. What did the 'superhero' Snooky have written on his costume? *(Be cool, save our fuel!)*
10. What did Snooky say to Lewis? *(He had to remember to turn everything off when he wasn't using them so that he could save fuel.)*

Getting the message – what can I do about it?
You can help in lots of ways:
- Like Lewis, you can remember to turn things off.
- Ask your family if you can all go out for walks or bike rides more, rather than using the car all the time. It's healthier, doesn't use any fuel and it's fun!
- Instead of wearing thin clothes and having the heating high, wear warmer clothes and have the heating at a lower setting.
- Ask your mums and dads to replace light bulbs with low energy ones – that just means they don't use as much fuel.
- If you don't do it already, start recycling things so that factories use less fuel because they'll be making less things.

Learning more
If you want to learn more about saving energy there are lots and lots of websites that will give you information – www.powerhousekids.com; www.oxfam.org.uk/coolplanet; www.recyclenow.com; are just a few. We all need to know about how to help look after our world, but knowing about it isn't enough! We have all got to learn to actually do things like switching lights and electrical things off and walking more! We must try and make them part of our daily routine so that they become habits and we don't even have to think about them!

Non-interactive Follow-up

Summary
- Energy is the ability to work.
- We need food to give us energy.
- Lots of things need energy – TVs, computers, washing machines, dishwashers, cookers, cars.
- Coal, oil and gas are fossil fuels.
- They are non-renewable forms of fuel.
- Lewis had lots of toys and electrical equipment.
- He looked for his hamster, Snooky, under the bed.
- 'Superhero' Snooky said, 'Be cool, save our fuel!'
- Snooky told Lewis to turn things off when he wasn't using them in order to save energy.

Reflection
It doesn't matter how young or old you are – you can help to save your mum and dad's energy bills and save fuel for other people who aren't born yet. After all, they'll want to be warm too and they'll want to have computers and televisions, won't they?

Prayer
Lord God,
Thank you that you have provided the fuels we need, which in turn provide energy for us to live our lives comfortably. Help us to realise that we have to save that energy for people in the future. Help us to remember to turn things off when we're not using them and to walk more so that we are helping to save fuel for everyone.
Amen.

10 Animals in Danger 1
Dolphins

Objective
To raise awareness of the way dolphins can become hurt and killed unnecessarily, and how steps can be taken to avoid this.

Links
Citizenship
2a: to research, discuss and debate topical issues, problems and events
2b: why and how rules and laws are made and enforced, why different rules are needed in different situations and how to take part in making and changing rules
2h: to recognise the role of voluntary, community and pressure groups

Props
A large can of tuna and a picture of a dolphin, or projected film of dolphins swimming in the sea.
A long skipping or other rope.
You'll need some volunteers to be 3 dolphins, 6 tuna fish and two fishermen.

Introduction

I just love tuna fish, don't you? Here's a tin that I'm going to be having for my tea. I can't make my mind up whether to make a yummy tuna salad or a huge tuna sandwich: maybe you can help me decide later. Anyway, we're not here to talk about what I'm having for tea – I want to tell you about how this can of tuna is not only good to eat, but it's also helping to save some very important lives around the world.

Story: Rafael the dolphin
Rafael was a dolphin. He lived in the beautiful clear, warm waters of the Pacific Ocean not far from Mexico. He loved to swim and play with his friends, Juanita and Miguel, and enjoyed larking about just like you do. Rafael, Juanita and Miguel used to chase each other about in the sea and sometimes they would jump right out of the water in huge great leaps, just for fun.

One day, when the three friends were out playing, Rafael noticed a big boat way out on the horizon, but he didn't take much notice of it and went back to playing with Juanita and Miguel. Today they were having a competition to see who could jump the highest out of the water. It was a bit annoying, as a huge shoal of tuna fish were getting in their way. A 'shoal' is the name of a big group of fish that swim around together. Whenever one of the dolphins tried to do an extra big leap, there always seemed to be a silly tuna fish right in the way. Rafael was just beginning to get cross, and had decided to try to find a quieter bit of ocean to play in with his friends, when he turned his head. From away in the distance, the dolphins heard a noise: chug-chug-chug-chug. Two smaller boats were coming towards them from where the big boat was.

The three friends stopped their leaping game and watched the boats coming closer. They had seen boats with people in before. Usually, the people were holding cameras and liked to take pictures of the dolphins as they played. Rafael loved to show off his best tricks when he was being watched and photographed. He was just getting ready to do some of his best leaps for the cameras, when he noticed that the men on the boats didn't have cameras but there was a big net stretched between the two boats. He had no idea what that could be for.

Let's have some of you up here to show everybody what was happening. I need three people to be the dolphins – I'll have three girls, please… *(keeping sexes separate makes identification easier for audience)* Thank you, girls. Now I need six boys to come and be tuna fish… OK, you boys stand over here. Now I need a couple of people to be the fisherman. *(Arrange the children, so that the boys and girls (tuna and dolphins) 'swim' around, and are then gradually herded into a group by the two fishermen and 'caught', using the long skipping rope as a net, and describe the process.)*

The fishermen wanted to catch the tuna fish, to sell for us to eat, but they didn't want to catch the dolphins. Who can tell me what happened, though? Hands up if you can work it out. *(wait for answers)* That's right: because the dolphins happened to be swimming in the same part of the sea as the tuna fish, they got tangled up in the nets too.

As it happened, the fishermen's nets had a big hole in, so Rafael, Miguel and Juanita got away that time, but not all dolphins are that lucky and many do get killed by accident.

INTERACTIVE FOLLOW-UP

Questions
1) Can you remember what sort of animals Rafael and his friends were? Hands up to answer. *(dolphins)*
2) Dolphins love playing games. Can you remember what game they were trying to play that day? Two of these answers are wrong, but one is right. You need to make a cross with your fingers for the wrong answers and give me a thumbs-up for the right answer. Were the dolphins:
   a. playing chase (X)
   b. playing hide and seek (X)
   c. seeing who could jump the highest out of the water (✓)
3) Someone was getting in the way of their game, though: what type of animal was that, I wonder? This time, give me a thumbs-up for the right answer and a big thumbs-down for the wrong answers. So, the animals that got in the way of Rafael's game, were they:
   a. whales (X)
   b. tuna fish (✓)
   c. fish fingers (X)

Getting the message
- What did the fishermen want that day? Hands up to tell me, please. *(They wanted to catch tuna.)*
- Can you tell me how they caught the fish? *(They used a net to catch them.)*
- Did the fishermen want to catch the dolphins? *(No, they were just in the way and got caught by accident.)*

Learning more
People love to eat tuna fish, but no one likes to eat dolphins and no one wants to hurt them. Sadly, many dolphins get caught up in tuna fishing nets and get killed by accident. Luckily, many countries have decided to try to stop this and there are rules about what types of nets fishermen are allowed to use. They should use different sorts of nets that don't trap dolphins in them. If you check the label before you buy a tin of tuna at the supermarket, you can tell if it's been caught by a fisherman who is trying to stop dolphins being killed by accident in his nets. Look for a little stamp on the label that says 'dolphin friendly' and you'll know that no dolphins have been hurt or killed along with the tuna fish.

NON-INTERACTIVE FOLLOW-UP

Summary
- Rafael, Miguel and Juanita are three dolphins who live in the Pacific Ocean, near Mexico.
- They like to play games and leap in and out of the water for fun.
- Sometimes people take pictures of them leaping and playing.
- One day, they were playing in the same area as a big shoal of tuna fish were swimming.
- Two fishing boats come along and put out nets to catch the tuna fish.
- The dolphins got caught up in the nets with the tuna fish.
- This time, the dolphins escaped through some holes in the nets but often dolphins get hurt and killed in this way.
- Many countries are trying to stop dolphins being killed and have made important rules to make fishermen use safer nets to catch 'dolphin friendly' tuna.
- Many cans of tuna are now labelled with the 'dolphin friendly' logo, so we can decide to buy tuna that has not harmed any dolphins.

Reflection
Imagine you are in a supermarket, helping to do the shopping. You need some tuna and there are two different types on the shelf: one is the 'dolphin friendly' type, but it costs a few pence more than a can that doesn't have the 'dolphin friendly' sign on it. Which one would you buy?

Prayer
Dear Lord,
Thank you for the world that you have given us: it's full of animals you've put there for us to eat and keep us healthy, like tuna fish, and animals like dolphins that are such fun to watch. Help us to think carefully about how we look after all the animals in the world and please help us to do what we can to stop animals being killed and hurt by accident.
Amen.

11 Animals in Danger 2
Tibetan Antelopes

Objective
To raise awareness of the way that some animals are endangered by poaching and of the way authorities, pressure groups and individuals are attempting to stop them.

Links
Citizenship
2a: to research, discuss and debate topical issues, problems and events
2b: why and how rules and laws are made and enforced, why different rules are needed in different situations and how to take part in making and changing rules
2h: to recognise the role of voluntary, community and pressure groups

Props
A thin shawl made of wool, silk or something similar.

INTRODUCTION

Do you like this shawl? I've bought it for my auntie, as she loves beautiful clothes and enjoys dressing up when she goes out. It was quite expensive, but nowhere near as expensive as the shawl I'm going to tell you about in this story. Listen carefully and you'll be amazed…

Story: Mariella the film star

Mariella was a famous film star - she had been in lots and lots of films. Because she was so famous and everybody loved to see her films, she was also very, VERY rich. Like some very rich people, she was also a bit spoiled. She could afford to buy just about anything she fancied and would sulk terribly if she couldn't get exactly what she wanted.

She loved clothes and wanted a new soft shawl to go with one of her posh dresses. She had heard of wonderful shawls made from very special wool, called shahtoosh, and she decided that she just HAD to have one.

Shahtoosh is wool that comes from a very rare antelope that lives high in the mountains of China, India and Tibet. It is the softest, warmest wool you could possibly imagine and it only grows on a special antelope called a Chiru. The name 'shahtoosh' means 'king of wools'. Now, who can tell me what other sorts of animals give us wool? *(Wait for answers.)* That's right. Sheep have long woolly coats, don't they? Does anyone know how we get the wool from the sheep? *(Again, wait for answers.)* Yes – a shearer carefully cuts the wool off the sheep in springtime, a bit like giving it a shave or a hair cut. The sheep might wriggle a bit, but being shorn doesn't hurt and it usually feels much better once the big heavy winter fleece has gone. A sheep's coat grows back again the next winter, so it can keep giving us wool every year of its life, without coming to any harm. Sadly, this isn't the same for the poor Chiru antelopes.

The special shahtoosh wool can't be shorn off the Chiru like sheep's wool. To get the wool, the Chiru need to be killed and the wool has to be scraped off their skins, which is not very nice at all. The Chiru live ever so high up in the mountains, where it is always very cold, so the wool is difficult to get. If it weren't the softest, warmest wool in the world, nobody would bother trying to get it but, because it is so special, people are willing to pay an awful lot of money for it. Mariella – remember the rich film star at the beginning of the story – was willing to pay £5,000 for a single shawl!

Because so many rich people want the beautiful shawls made of shahtoosh, and will happily pay a great deal of money for them, lots of people hunt the Chiru. It takes the wool of many Chiru to make just one shawl and this is causing a big problem. More Chiru are being killed than are being born, so very soon there won't be any of these beautiful animals left.

When animals are in danger of being hunted so much that there won't be any left at all, we say that they are 'endangered'. There are people who care so much about endangered animals, that they spend their time trying to save them and stop the hunting. They go to the governments and people in charge of the countries where animals like the Chiru live and try to persuade them to make hunting them against the law. This doesn't stop all of the hunting but at least it means that, if the hunters are caught, they can be put into prison and punished. That should put many of the hunters off and save the Chiru from becoming extinct, or dying out altogether.

Remember our film star, Mariella? Well, she heard about the danger the Chiru are in and decided not to have a shahtoosh shawl after all. Let's give her a big cheer!

INTERACTIVE FOLLOW-UP

Questions
1) Who can remember what the special wool from the antelope is called? Hands up if you think it is:
   a. Shootash
   b. Shahtoosh (✓)
   c. Atishoo
2) Why do you think the wool is called 'the king of wools'? *(On account of the superior quality of its warmth and softness.)*
3) How is shahtoosh different from ordinary sheep's wool? *(It cannot be shorn off, but needs to be scraped off the dead animals' skins.)*
4) Why are the shahtoosh endangered? *(It takes the wool from several Chiru to make just one shawl, so more Chiru are being killed than can be replaced by the diminishing herds.)*
5) What are people doing to stop this happening? *(Pressure groups are lobbying governments, who are outlawing the hunting of Chiru and trade in shahtoosh.)*

Getting the message
Some people think that, as long as they have enough money, they should be allowed to buy anything they want. What do you think? Put your thumbs up if you agree with them and put your thumbs down if you think that it's more important to look after rare animals.

It is illegal to hunt Chiru for their wool. Who knows what 'illegal' means?

Learning more
Governments have made hunting Chiru illegal and they put the hunters and shawl-makers in prison if they catch them. Can you think of any other ways that people could help the Chiru from becoming extinct? *(Pressure groups can tell people all about it – raise awareness – and individuals can decide not to buy illegally manufactured shawls and so kill the market.)*

NON-INTERACTIVE FOLLOW-UP

Summary
- A famous, very rich film star decides that she wants a shawl made of very special, expensive wool.
- The wool, called shahtoosh, comes from the Chiru antelope that live high in the mountains of China, India and Tibet.
- It cannot be shorn, like sheep's wool, but must be scraped off the dead animals' skins.
- The Chiru are being hunted near to extinction.
- Pressure groups have succeeded in making the hunting of Chiru and the manufacture of shawls illegal.
- People who break the laws are punished by being put into prison.

Reflection
There are lots of things in this world that we would love to be able to have. Some things we can have, without doing any harm. Some things, like shawls made of shahtoosh, are lovely to have but we risk making the Chiru antelope extinct – so there won't be any more Chiru, anywhere in the world, any more. What would be more important to you: having a lovely soft shawl or knowing that the world still has a beautiful, rare animal enjoying its life in a wild place?

Prayer
Dear Lord,
Thank you that you have filled our world with beautiful and precious things. Please help us not to be selfish about the things we want. Help us not to mind doing without things that will bring harm or suffering to places, animals or people that you have made.
Amen.

12 Animals in Danger 3
The Giant Panda

Objective
To help children to understand why the giant panda is an endangered animal and what is being done to protect it.

Links
Citizenship
2e: to realise that people and other living things have needs, and that they have responsibilities to meet them

Props
A teddy bear, a picture of a giant panda and a map or globe showing the position of China (none of these is essential).

INTRODUCTION

I wonder which wild animal is the easiest to recognise in the whole world? Maybe a giraffe or an elephant or a snake. Or maybe it's another one? Today's assembly is all about an animal that everyone knows but hardly anyone has ever seen in the wild.

Story: The Giant Panda
Everyone seems to like bears – that's why teddy bears are so popular. A long time ago, there used to be wild bears in this country, but they were all hunted and killed. There are still brown and black bears living in the mountains and forests of countries like Canada and Russia. And you probably know that big white polar bears live in the snowy arctic. But what is the rarest bear in the world, the one that hardly anyone has ever seen in the wild?

The answer is the giant panda. It's very easy to recognise a panda because of its black and white fur, and you may have seen a panda in a zoo, but did you know that there are only about 600 pandas living in the wild, in the whole world? This means that pandas are in danger of dying out altogether unless people take great care to protect them.

Giant pandas are only found in one place in the world: in the mountains in one far corner of China. They usually live alone and spend nearly all their time either eating or asleep. Pandas have to eat a lot because just about their only food is a very tall grass called bamboo. There's not much goodness in a piece of bamboo, pandas have to eat about 24 kilograms of it each day – that weighs the same as 370 Mars Bars! They also spend about 14 hours eating each day.

But why are pandas so rare – why aren't there more of them in the world? The reason is that the bamboo forest where they live in the mountains of China is gradually being chopped down by people. There are over a thousand million people living in China and they need lots of wood – for firewood, for making furniture and houses, for instance. They also need to grow a lot of food to feed everyone, so farmers are always cutting down trees to make more land to grow rice and other plants.

All this means that there is less space for pandas to live in and each panda needs a very big area of forest to find enough bamboo to eat. There is another reason that pandas are dying out too – they have been hunted and trapped by people. Because pandas are so rare, their fur is very valuable. The Chinese government and police have tried to stop this and hunters can be put in prison for killing a panda, but it is very hard to catch them in the mountains.

So, how can we stop this beautiful animal from being lost forever? One answer is to capture a few pandas without hurting them and to put them in a zoo. This might sound unkind, but pandas can easily be protected and cared for in a zoo. If a female panda has a baby, or cub, then, when it grows up, the panda can be released into the wild. Several zoos around the world have tried to do this, but pandas don't seem to like having babies in zoos.

At least today enough people in China and in countries everywhere care about pandas to try to protect them by keeping their forests safe. Perhaps, one day in the future, the giant panda might not be the rarest bear in the world.

INTERACTIVE FOLLOW-UP

Questions
1) Why has hardly anyone seen a giant panda in the wild? *(They are very rare; they live in a remote part of China that is hard to visit; they live alone high in the mountains.)*
2) Why are there so few giant pandas left in the world? *(Their habitat has been lost – over 50% of Chinese bamboo forests have been cut down in the last 30 years; they have been hunted and trapped; they only live in one small part of the world.)*
3) What is being done to save the giant panda from dying out altogether? *(The species is now protected; there are laws against hunting pandas; there are breeding programmes in zoos, although these have not been very successful.)*

Getting the message
Half of the giant pandas' bamboo forests in China have been cut down since your parents were born. What can be done to stop this happening? *(Help the local farmers so that they do not need to clear the land to grow crops; supply them with wood from other places; guard the forests; send money to organisations which help to protect endangered species.)*

Let's see what you know about pandas. True or false? Put your thumb up or down:
- A panda is a type of bear. *(T)*
- Pandas are brown and white. *(F)*
- All wild giant pandas live in the forests and mountains of China. *(T)*
- Female pandas have lots of babies called cubs. *(F – they only have one cub usually)*
- Some pandas are kept in zoos to protect them. *(T)*
- Pandas could die out altogether if their bamboo forests are cut down. *(T)*

Learning more

There are excellent videos of pandas in the wild at (www.arkive.org) – the website also has information about other endangered species around the world.

NON-INTERACTIVE FOLLOW-UP

Summary
- The giant panda is the rarest bear in the world and an endangered species.
- There are estimated to be just 600 pandas living in the wild.
- Giant pandas are only found in remote mountains in western China, where there are bamboo forests.
- Pandas eat bamboo almost exclusively and must eat huge amounts of it because it is nutritionally poor food.
- Panda numbers have decreased because of habitat loss due to deforestation for timber, firewood and farming – land is under pressure because of China's vast population.
- Pandas are protected but they are still occasionally hunted. There is a zoo breeding programme but pandas rarely breed in captivity (and only have one cub).

Reflection

The giant panda is one of the most beautiful and rare animals in the world and one of the most easily recognised. It would be a terrible tragedy if the giant panda were to die out. We all need to care for the animals of our planet – to look after the places they live and not to harm them in any way. Think what a dull place the world would be without amazing and wonderful animals like the giant panda.

Prayer

Dear Lord,

Thank you for all the wonderful and amazing animals in the world, including the giant panda. Help us to protect these rare and gentle creatures. Please Lord, help people to look after the bamboo forests where they live and not to cut down the trees there. Thank you for every living creature on our beautiful planet.

Amen.

13 Animals in Danger 4
Tigers

Objective
To raise children's awareness of the plight of tigers and what is being done to help protect them.

Links
Citizenship/PSHE
2a: to research, discuss and debate topical issues, problems and events
2h: to recognise the role of voluntary, community and pressure groups

Props
Images of tigers to show or project, if possible the 5 different subspecies: Bengal, Indochinese, Chinese, Siberian and Sumatran.
Globe or world map to show where tigers live.

Introduction

Did you know that kangaroos can't move backwards? Did you know that elephants are the only animals that can't jump? And did you know that tigers have striped skin as well as striped fur? Who thinks that all those things are false? *(Invite responses.)* Well, you're wrong! They're all true! But going back to tigers – they're in trouble.

What's happening to the tigers?
Hands up if you think there's only one type of tiger? Well, if you didn't put your hand up you're… right! There are actually five different kinds of tiger in the world – there used to be eight but three are now extinct. Who can tell me what extinct means? *(Invite responses.)* That's right – it means they don't exist any more, which is terrible, isn't it? *(Show images if you have them at this point and map to show where tigers live.)*

Tigers are truly magnificent animals aren't they? But they have suffered terribly because they have been hunted and also a lot of the forests where they live have been destroyed. Why do you think tigers have stripes (and by the way, did you know that no two tigers have the same stripes)? *(Invite responses.)* Their stripes hide them from their prey but, because their habitats are being lost, they can't hide themselves and that means they can't catch the food they need to survive. All of this means that the tigers that are still around are in danger of becoming extinct, like the other three kinds.

This is a true story about a little girl who was so upset when she found out at school about what was happening to tigers that she decided to do something.

Story: Molly holds a party

Molly and her friends were learning about the differences between countries at school. It was one of Molly's favourite lessons – she loved hearing about the different animals, food, clothes and how schools were different. When she closed her eyes, she could imagine all the bright colours of an Indian market and all the animals like elephants, monkeys wandering in the streets and brightly coloured birds like parrots, just flying around! One day, her teacher told the children that they were going to learn about endangered animals in India and that one in particular was in great danger – the tiger. Molly listened to her teacher tell them that tigers were being hunted so much that their numbers were becoming less and less; she also said that, because so many forests were being destroyed, the tigers couldn't hide themselves from their prey and so they were going hungry and dying of starvation. The last thing Molly's teacher said in the lesson was, 'Remember endangered means there's still time! Extinct means gone forever!'

All the way home Molly thought hard. Her teacher had told them that there were organisations that were helping to save tigers –maybe she could help too! Even though it was her birthday the next day, she couldn't stop thinking about the tigers. That night, Molly asked her dad to help her look for information about tigers and, sure enough, they found lots of websites just about saving tigers. The more Molly and her dad read, the more worried Molly got. 'Do you know, Dad,' she said, 'the best birthday present I could have would be that tigers weren't endangered any more!' Then Molly had a brilliant idea! 'Dad,' she said, 'can I have a birthday party for tigers?'

Molly's dad looked at her. 'Well, you know we'd arranged to go bowling. But that can easily be changed.' So, Molly and her parents invited her friends to a 'Save the tiger' party! They had striped cloths, napkins cups and plates. She had a tiger birthday cake and the sandwiches were made with tiger bread (you can actually buy that at the supermarket - look out for it!). Instead of giving her birthday presents, Molly asked her friends to donate money to the 'Save the Tiger Fund', which they did. Altogether she raised over £100!

What a great idea for a party! I think Molly was very kind, don't you?

INTERACTIVE FOLLOW-UP

Questions

1) How many different types of tiger are there? *(five)*
2) How many types are extinct? *(three)*
3) Why do tigers have stripes? *(for camouflage)*
4) What's special about tiger's stripes? *(no two tigers' stripes are the same)*
5) Why are tigers endangered? *(hunting and loss of habitat)*
6) What does their loss of habitat mean for the tiger? *(They can't hide from their prey, which means it's much more difficult for them to catch their food.)*
7) What was Molly learning about at school? *(differences between countries; endangered animals – the tiger)*
8) What did Molly do when she got home? *(she found out as much as she could about tigers)*
9) What did Molly decide to do? *(have a 'Save the Tiger' birthday)*
10) Did Molly get any presents? *(No, she asked people to give money to the 'Save the Tiger' fund instead.)*

Getting the message – what can I do about it?

Tigers only live for 10 to 15 years, which is quite a short time, and there are now less than 7,000 tigers left in the world, which is very few. There is now a law which bans anyone from killing tigers but not everyone obeys it, which means that the tigers are still in danger. If you're interested in learning more about tigers and what you can do to help, visit the website of the World Wildlife Fund (www.wwf.org.uk) or (www.kidsfortigers.org). When you've learnt a lot about tigers – tell others! Telling other people about the dangers tigers face is an important part of changing things! Remember – endangered means there is still time, extinct means gone forever!

Learning more

Tigers are excellent swimmers! They love going for a dip in the water if it gets too hot, which it does very often in the areas where they live. Would you fancy having a swim with a tiger? They hunt at night, usually on their own, and they are also the largest members of the cat family. Tigers are very interesting creatures, as well as being magnificent to look at.

NON-INTERACTIVE FOLLOW-UP

Summary

- Tigers have striped skin as well as striped fur.
- There are 5 different kinds of tigers left.
- There were 8, but 3 are now extinct.
- No two tigers have the same stripes.
- They are endangered through loss of habitat and hunting.
- Tigers love swimming and often take a dip when it's too hot.
- They are the largest member of the cat family.
- They hunt at night, on their own.

Reflection

The Caspian, Java and Bali tigers only exist now in pictures. The other kinds of tigers are in danger of becoming extinct too. If you and your family can help organisations to protect them through adopting an animal or giving what you can afford, that is great. All of us should care about what happens to the animals on our planet.

Prayer

Lord God,
We are sad that some of the beautiful tigers you made no longer exist. We pray that the people who hunt and destroy them will be stopped and that the rest of the tiger population will continue to grow.
Amen.

14 ANIMALS IN DANGER 5
The Green Sea Turtle

Objective
To raise children's awareness of the green sea turtle as an endangered species and of the role of pressure groups and voluntary organisations in supporting them.

Links
Citizenship/PSHE
2a: to research, discuss and debate topical issues, problems and events
2h: to recognise the role of voluntary, community and pressure groups

Props
(not essential)
Images of green sea turtles.
Images of Cayman Islands.
Globe to show position of Cayman Islands.

INTRODUCTION

Did you know that a butterfly tastes things with its feet? Isn't that strange? Just imagine using your feet to eat your cornflakes! This morning we're going to learn about a butterfly and a turtle who were great friends.

Story: Timmy the cross-eyed turtle
Timmy was a green sea turtle who lived in the sea grass in a small bay in the Cayman Islands, which was absolutely beautiful. *(Show images at this point if you have them.)* Timmy loved getting up in the morning and wandering down to the sea to have his regular breakfast of shrimps and jellyfish. He lived with his mother, two brothers, Henry and Freddie, and his sister, Lottie, who were actually quite nasty to Timmy. Do you know why? Well, Timmy was a very handsome turtle BUT he was cross-eyed. It didn't mean that he couldn't see, but it did mean that he looked different to his brothers and sister, and I'm afraid they made fun of him rather a lot.

As I said, he could see perfectly well, but sometimes, when he was walking, he moved diagonally rather than straight ahead. So he quite often found himself somewhere that he hadn't intended to go to. But even that didn't matter because it meant that he often found new places to catch his shrimps and jellyfish that the others didn't know about. Timmy didn't mind because his friend, Leonardo, who was a butterfly, was usually with him anyway. Butterflies often land on turtle's noses to feed from their tears, and turtles cry a lot – not because they're sad but because their tears protect them from the sand when they're digging. His brothers and sister got very annoyed with Leonardo and his friends because, when the butterflies landed on their noses, it made them go cross-eyed. But, of course, that didn't matter to Timmy because he was cross-eyed anyway! So he and Leonardo had great fun together and were great friends.

One day, Leonardo and Timmy decided to go and get their breakfast as usual and, because Timmy went a bit more diagonally than usual, they ended up in a part of the bay that they hadn't been to before. Timmy was excited by this because it probably meant more shrimps and maybe some extra big jellyfish. 'I think you'd better take extra care here, Timmy,' said Leonardo. 'Some men were here yesterday, you never know what they'll leave around.'

'Don't worry,' said Timmy cheerfully. 'I'll be careful. You keep watch for the others.'

No sooner had he said that than his brothers and sister arrived and rushed (as much as a turtle can rush) past him, saying, 'Yeah, Timmy. You thought you were going to get all the shrimps – but WE are!'

Timmy sighed and let them go past him. He was used to them being nasty. 'Come on, Timmy,' said Leonardo, who was sitting on his nose as usual. 'Let's go somewhere else.'

'OK', said Timmy, and he turned to go what he thought was straight on but he actually went diagonally into the sea! As he went in, he saw something moving in the water which wasn't a shrimp. It looked like a net! Not only that but his brothers and sister were swimming towards it! If he didn't warn them, they would get entangled in the net and die! But what could he do? 'Leonardo – look, look at that net! They're all going to get caught up in it. They can't see it from where they are because the sun's shining on it and they won't listen to me. Not only that, I can't get to them in time.'

Leonardo fluttered round and saw what Timmy meant. 'Don't worry,' he said, I'll fly over and warn them.' So Leonardo fluttered over to where Timmy's eldest brother, Henry, was swimming and landed on his nose to warn him.

'Get off me, you nuisance!' shouted Henry. 'Haven't I told you before to leave me alone? Go on, get lost. I'm busy.'

Leonardo pulled himself to his full height (which wasn't much, but it gave him more courage) and said in his sternest voice, 'Now just you listen to me, Henry. Timmy has seen a shrimp net that you're all swimming towards – if you don't turn round now, you'll all die!' Leonardo fluttered back to Timmy and Henry stopped swimming. He strained his eyes and, sure enough, he could just see the net on the glittering water and he was very, very close.

He turned round immediately and shouted to his brother and sister, 'Stop! Stop! There's a net!' They all managed to stop just in time and swam to the shore. Timmy and Leonardo were waiting for them. Leonardo was on Timmy's nose, but he was facing them rather than Timmy. Henry, Freddie and Lottie moved very slowly towards them both and Henry spoke first. 'Timmy and Leonardo, we're very sorry for being so mean to you. You saved our lives! I'll never mind you landing on my nose again and, Timmy, will you forgive us for being so horrible?'

'Oh yes! Please forgive us,' said Freddie and Lottie as well.

' 'Course I will,' said Timmy. And off they all went to find a different part of the beach to have their breakfast together. And Timmy's brothers and sister never made fun of his cross-eyed eyes again.

INTERACTIVE FOLLOW-UP

Questions

1) How do butterflies taste? *(with their feet)*
2) Where did Timmy live? *(in sea grass in a bay in the Cayman Islands)*
3) How many brothers and sisters did he have? *(two brothers and one sister)*
4) What did Timmy usually have for breakfast? *(shrimps and jellyfish)*
5) How did Timmy move occasionally? *(diagonally)*
6) Who was Leonardo? *(a butterfly who was Timmy's friend)*
7) What did Leonardo feed from? *(Timmy's tears)*
8) Why do turtles cry a lot? *(to protect their eyes from the sand whilst they're digging)*
9) What did Timmy see in the water that was dangerous? *(a shrimp net)*
10) Why was the shrimp net dangerous? *(because the turtles could get entangled in it and die)*
11) How did the other turtles manage to avoid swimming into the net? *(Leonardo landed on Henry's nose and warned them)*
12) What did Henry say after they came out of the water? *(he apologised to Timmy and Leonardo)*

Getting the message – what can I do about it?

Did you know that sea turtles are one of the Earth's most ancient creatures? Who can tell me what ancient means? *(very, very old)* They have been on the Earth far longer than human beings and there are seven different types of turtle. Isn't it terrible that these creatures which have been on the Earth for so long are now endangered? Who can tell me what endangered means? *(It means that there are so few left that they are in danger of becoming extinct.)*

They actually do spend most of their lives in the water, because moving on the land is quite awkward for them *(show images again if you have them)*. These lovely creatures are endangered for quite a few reasons. We heard about one reason in the story – can anyone remember what that was? *(entangling themselves in shrimp nets)* They are also in danger because people take their eggs, so fewer baby turtles are being born. Another reason is all the pollution or poisonous waste that is being put into the oceans, which is harmful to them.

You can help protect animals that are in danger even if they live far away. There are lots of different charities that give you the chance to adopt an animal and support their work. Ask your mums and dads to help you look for information about them on the internet. The World Wildlife Fund works to help all different types of animals in danger and there are many others that are working just for turtles! You can also remember not to throw litter into the sea and recycle as much as you can so that less waste is put into the oceans.

Learning more

Most sea turtles live for between 15 and 20 years, and some may live until they are 80 years old! Can you remember the food Timmy and his brothers and sister ate? *(shrimps and jellyfish)* That's right and sometimes turtles can mistake plastic bags that have been put into the water for jellyfish – if they swallow them, they die. They don't just eat shrimps and jellyfish – they also eat seaweed, crabs, snails and other small sea creatures. Although the sea turtle is in danger, there are lots of organisations that are trying to help preserve them.

Non-interactive Follow-up

Summary

- Butterflies taste with their feet.
- Sea turtles live in sea grass in small bays and coves. Timmy lived in the Cayman Islands.
- They eat shrimps, jellyfish, seaweed, crabs and other sea creatures.
- Timmy had two brothers *(Henry and Freddie)* and one sister *(Lottie)*.
- Timmy was cross-eyed, which made him move diagonally sometimes.
- His best friend was Leonardo, a butterfly who balanced on his nose and fed on his tears.
- Turtles cry a lot because their tears protect their eyes from the sand.
- Timmy saw a shrimp net in the water that his brothers and sister couldn't see because of the sun.
- Leonardo flew to Henry and warned him.
- Henry, Freddie and Lottie asked Timmy and Leonardo to forgive them for being nasty to them.
- Turtles can live to be 80 years old.
- They are endangered because of fishing nets, hunting and pollution.

Reflection

Turtles are gentle creatures that have lived on the Earth for a very long time. All of the different kinds of turtle, except one, are now listed as endangered. We should all care about what happens to animals because we don't want them just to exist in picture books or in films in the future.

Prayer

Lord God,
Thank you for all the different kinds of animals you have put on the Earth. Thank you also for all the different organisations that are trying to protect animals which are endangered or threatened. Help us to find out how we can help too.
Amen.

15 Animals in Danger 6
The Blue Whale

Objective
To raise children's awareness of the blue whale as an endangered species and of the role of pressure groups and voluntary organisations in supporting them.

Links
Citizenship/PSHE
2a: to research, discuss and debate topical issues, problems and events
2h: to recognise the role of voluntary, community and pressure groups

Props
Images of blue whales to project or show.

INTRODUCTION

(Show the images of the blue whale.) This is the largest creature on Earth. It is over 32 metres long. *(Give comparisons that children can relate to, e.g. twice the length of the school hall; the same length as the school field.)* Does anyone know what it is? *(Invite responses.)* That's right, it's a blue whale. It is AMAZINGLY big. Did you know that its heart is the same size as a VW Beetle car? That's a big heart! It is a beautiful, shy creature but it is in danger. Why is it in danger? Let's listen to this story which will give us some clues.

Story: Boris and Doris
Boris and Doris the blue whales were heading off towards warmer waters because it was getting a bit chilly for them as it was winter time. They enjoyed themselves diving and coming up for air and swimming along happily. Occasionally they had a race, but Doris usually won (she was a bit bigger than Boris) so they didn't do that too often because Boris sulked. But Doris did like winning races so she said to Boris, 'Come on, let's race one more time.'

Boris grunted and said, 'OK then,' although he was feeling a bit tired. Doris charged off as usual and Boris thought he might as well let her get on with it, so he changed direction for a while and headed off after some tasty shrimps he'd noticed. They would do as a starter anyway. Doris had also changed direction and was ahead of him. (She knew he'd be after the shrimps.) So she headed back to meet him. As she was speeding along, she saw a net dangling in the distance with Boris swimming leisurely towards it. He was swimming with his eyes closed for a lark, which he often did.

'Oh no,' thought Doris. 'He'll get tangled up in the net!' Boris obviously couldn't see her or the net because he had his eyes closed, so the only thing she could do was yell – which she did. Blue whales make the loudest noise of any animal on the Earth – they are even louder than a jet engine! 'BORIS,' she yelled. 'STOP! YOU'RE HEADING STRAIGHT FOR A NET!'

Boris opened his eyes with a start; he'd been having a lovely daydream about the rest of his dinner. Then he saw the net! He just managed to brake and turn round before he got caught in it! Phew! He'd heard lots of stories about his uncles and cousins being caught up in nets, but he'd always managed to avoid them. But this time he nearly didn't – if it hadn't been for Doris, he would have been tangled up himself. When they met up, he said, 'Thanks Doris, that was a close shave!'

'Humph,' said Doris. 'Perhaps you'll stop that daft habit of swimming with your eyes closed now! Let's get to those warm waters as quickly as possible and you'll have to wait for your supper.' And off they went.

INTERACTIVE FOLLOW-UP

Questions

1) What kind of creatures are blue whales? *(They are the largest creatures on Earth and they are very shy.)*
2) How big are their hearts? *(The same size as a VW Beetle car.)*
3) Where were Boris and Doris heading? *(They were going to warmer waters.)*
4) What did Doris want to do? *(She wanted to have a race.)*
5) What did Boris do? *(He changed direction and was swimming with his eyes closed, dreaming about his dinner.)*
6) What did Doris do? *(She changed direction too, ahead of Boris.)*
7) What did Doris see? *(She saw Boris heading towards a fishing net with his eyes closed.)*
8) What did she do? *(She yelled at him to avoid the net.)*
9) What's special about the noise a blue whale makes? *(They are the loudest creatures on Earth – louder than a jet engine!)*
10) What is one of the reasons that blue whales are endangered? *(They get entangled in fishing nets.)*

Getting the message – what can I do about it?

Well, Boris had a lucky escape, didn't he? What do you think one of the reasons might be that blue whales are endangered? *(Lots of them have got tangled up in nets.)* That's right, but there are some other reasons too. A big reason is that blue whales were hunted and captured by lots of people from 1930 to about 1960. By the time it got to 1960, they were nearly extinct. Who can tell me what extinct means? *(An animal is classed as extinct if it hasn't been seen in the wild for 50 years.)* At the moment, experts think there might be about 5,000 to 10,000 left – blue whales can be found in all the oceans of the world.

There are lots of things you can do to help animals like the blue whale that are endangered. Go on the website (www.wwf.org) which is a good place to start for finding out information about endangered animals and will give you lots of other links. You could draw a picture and write a letter to the Prime Minister telling him how worried you are; another important thing to do is telling people – the more people you tell, the more people will want to help!

Learning more

Everything about the blue whale is enormous. It is the largest animal on Earth, ever. Fifty people could stand on its tongue, its spout shoots up at least 30 feet when it comes up for air. Whales aren't fish either! They are mammals like you and me! That means they breathe with lungs (take a deep breath and feel your chest expand!). And they feed their babies with milk. Apart from being hunted and being entangled in nets, the other major threat to blue whales is pollution. All the waste that goes into the sea is harmful to all fish and marine life, not just whales. Make sure you put your rubbish in the right place and recycle as much as you can.

NON-INTERACTIVE FOLLOW-UP

Summary

- Blue whales are the largest creatures on Earth.
- They can grow up to 32 metres long and their hearts are the same size as a VW Beetle car.
- Blue whales are very shy.
- Boris and Doris were heading off to warmer waters because it was winter time.
- They decided to have a race and Boris went off on his own after some shrimps. He was swimming with his eyes closed.
- Doris saw the net and yelled to Boris to avoid it.
- Blue whales are the loudest creatures on Earth – they are louder than a jet engine.
- They are endangered because of fishing nets, hunting and pollution.
- They were brought to the brink of extinction because of hunting.
- It is estimated that there are between 5,000 and 10,000 blue whales left in the world.

Reflection

The blue whale is a magnificent creature that should be allowed to roam in the oceans as it was meant to do. The fact that it is so shy and harmless makes the fact that it is hunted even more terrible. We can help protect these creatures by making sure that we don't pollute beaches and by making sure that we cut down on our waste because lots of waste ends up in the sea, which harms the fish and marine animals that live there.

Prayer

Lord God,

Thank you for all the beautiful creatures that you have put on the Earth. We pray that the blue whale will not become extinct and that you will help organisations like the World Wildlife Fund to protect them and other animals that are endangered or threatened. Help us to help by thinking about our waste and by not adding to the pollution in the sea.

Amen.

16 Farming

Objective
For children to understand that there are different farming methods in the world and that organic farming is in harmony with the environment.

Links

Citizenship
1a: to talk and write about their opinions and explain their views on issues that affect themselves and society

Geography
5a: recognise how people can improve the environment

Props
A packet of seeds – preferably fairly large like courgettes or sunflower seeds which can be seen clearly

INTRODUCTION

Who can tell me what kinds of jobs there are in the world or what kinds of jobs your mums and dads do? *(Invite responses.)* That's a lot of different kinds of jobs! But did you know that there's one job that more people do than any other? Does anyone know what it is? *(farming)* There are more people who work as farmers in the world than do any other kind of job. There are also lots of different types of farms. More and more farmers are starting to farm organically in the world. But what does that mean? It means lots of things, but let's learn what farming's all about first.

Things that grow are a miracle!
Look at these seeds – they don't look very exciting do they? *(Pass them round.)* But they are! When they're not producing plants, they're what we call dormant or sleeping. But, when they have the right conditions, they wake up and burst into life – that's a miracle! Each seed has all the information inside it to know what it's going to grow into – it's got its own instruction manual!

Growing food is not easy. All farmers, all over the world, have to solve some big problems to make sure their plants can thrive and grow. They have to make sure the soil has enough goodness in it to feed little plants so they will grow to be healthy and good to eat. They have to control bugs and other pests that can attack and eat the plants. And they have to control weeds that can "choke" young plants by taking up the space, sunlight and nutrients they need to grow.

Many farmers solve these problems by using pesticides and chemicals which kill weeds but which cause pollution and are not healthy to have in the ground. Organic farmers are different because they try to solve the problems using nature's ways and without using chemicals. For instance, there are good bugs and bad bugs – organic farmers buy good bugs and release them into the fields to eat the bad bugs! Even though it takes more work, farming organically is the healthiest choice. Organic farming helps keep our air, soil, water and food supply clean. Organic farmers also provide their farm workers and neighbours with a healthier environment. Organic farming helps make healthy food and a healthy planet.

INTERACTIVE FOLLOW-UP

Questions
1) What is the job that most people do in the world? *(farming)*
2) What are seeds called when they're not growing? *(dormant)*
3) What kinds of problems do farmers have to overcome? *(weeds, making sure they have good soil, pests)*
4) What problems do pesticides cause? *(pollution and unhealthy environment)*
5) What do organic farmers use to control pests? *(they buy good bugs which eat the bad bugs)*
6) Why is organic farming healthier? *(It keeps the air, soil, water and food supply clean; gives farm workers and neighbours a healthy environment.)*

Getting the message – what can I do about it?
Organic farmers try very hard to make farming healthy and our food healthy – it makes sense and it makes a better world for all of us. It will especially help future generations – and that means you! So what you can do is learn all you can about eating healthily so you'll do the best for you and your family and the planet!

Learning more
There are thousands and thousands of insects that live on a farm. They can be helpful or harmful to the farm and its crops. Good bugs that help fight the bugs that eat crops are often called "beneficial insects". Other insects, like bees, help carry pollen from the flowers of plants to the flowers of other plants as they fly around. This is called pollination and it is needed for plants to reproduce – in other words, make more seeds.

NON-INTERACTIVE FOLLOW-UP

Summary
- More people work as farmers than any other job.
- Seeds that aren't growing are dormant.
- Farmers have to overcome lots of problems in order to grow crops – weeds, good soil, pests.
- Pesticides cause pollution and an unhealthy environment.
- Organic farmers use good bugs to eat up the bad bugs.
- Organic farming keeps the land, air, water and food supply clean. It creates a healthy environment for farm workers and neighbours.

Reflection
Organic farming works with the environment and avoids the use of synthetic pesticides or fertilisers. Sometimes organic food is more expensive than food grown by other farms, but lots of people don't mind paying more because they believe organic farming is more environmentally friendly, healthier and better for all of us.

Prayer
Lord God,
Thank you for the miracle of growth – it's hard to believe that a seed contains all the information it needs to grow into a healthy plant. Thank you for all the farmers who are choosing to farm organically and who are trying to make the world a better and healthier place to live.
Amen.

17 Health

Objective
To raise children's awareness of the necessity to eat healthily and to exercise regularly.

Links
Citizenship
3a: what makes a healthy lifestyle, including the benefits of exercise and healthy eating, what affects mental health, and how to make informed choices

Props
Football, tennis racquet, swimming goggles, cycling helmet, pair of trainers.

Statements to be projected as follows:
1. I eat lots of fresh fruit and vegetables every day *(at least 5 portions)*.
2. I eat some fruit and vegetables every day *(not as much as 5 portions)*.
3. I eat fruit and vegetables sometimes, not every day.
4. I eat lots of cakes, chocolate, sweets and chips.

Introduction

Can I have some volunteers please? *(Choose 5 children and give each of them one of the sporting props.)* Now we're going to have a look at what sports these children are going to do. *(Ask children to mime the sport that they have the prop for.)* Look at all this activity! What a bunch of healthy children! *(Ask the children to give you the props and then tell them to sit down.)* That's brilliant – let's just go through what they are. *(Hold the props up and ask children to name each sport.)* Who does any of these sports? Fantastic! Can you think of any other sports or games we can do? *(Invite responses.)* I'm very impressed. Today we're going to think about what makes us healthy and we've made a great start.

What keeps us healthy?
Why is it a good idea to do all these sports? *(exercise)* Why do we need to do exercise, then? *(to keep our bodies healthy)* Some people think that, if you exercise, you get tired but actually the opposite is true. Exercise gives you lots of energy and life is much more fun when you've got lots of energy. Exercise makes you feel happy! But do we just need to do lots of exercise to keep us healthy? *(No, we need to eat the right food as well.)* Let's look at these sentences and decide which apply to us. *(Project the quiz at this point.)*

What about the first question? *(Read it with the children.)* Who thinks they eat more than five portions of fruit and vegetables a day? *(Invite responses and take a show of hands, repeat with questions 2-4.)* Which is the healthiest of those statements? *(number 1)* People like doctors and health experts say that we should eat at least five portions of fruit and vegetables a day to keep healthy. Who can tell me what their favourite fruit is? *(Invite responses.)*

Excellent – so even if you don't eat five portions a day at the moment, who's going to try and do that from now on? Well done. If you're healthy, you're more likely to have lots of energy to do all your school work and to play as well. People who eat lots of fatty and sugary foods like cakes, sweets, biscuits and chips are more likely to be ill.

Who gets lots of sleep? That's great – children need lots of sleep as well as good food and exercise to keep healthy. So make sure you go to bed early as well - then you'll be super-healthy!

INTERACTIVE FOLLOW-UP

Questions
1) Why do we need to exercise? *(to keep our bodies healthy)*
2) Why else is exercise good for us? *(It gives you energy and makes you happy.)*
3) What else do we need to keep us healthy? *(Good food – at least 5 portions a day of fruit and vegetables, not too many sugary and fatty foods and plenty of sleep.)*
4) What is likely to happen to you if you eat lots of cakes and chips? *(You'll become ill.)*

Getting the message – what can I do about it?
Keeping healthy is easy – you only need to do 30 minutes of exercise every day to stay healthy, as well as eating properly. They're both equally important and, if you do what you should do, your heart will be healthy, your muscles will be strong and, most importantly, you'll feel great! When is the best time to be physically active? Again that's easy, anytime! In fact, let's all stand up now. *(Ask children to stand.)* We'll all run on the spot for a bit to get our hearts going! *(Keep this up for a few minutes and then ask the children to sit down.)* Well, that's five of your minutes done today already! Can you feel your heart beating faster – that's healthy; it means your heart is pumping more oxygen round your body so you feel more awake.

Learning more
Did you know that a quarter of the people in the world are ill because they don't have enough to eat and another quarter of the people are ill because they eat too much!

Non-interactive Follow-up

Summary
- We need to eat five portions of fruit and vegetables a day to keep healthy and not eat too many sugary and fatty foods.
- We need to exercise for at least 30 minutes every day to keep healthy.
- We need plenty of sleep.
- Exercise is good for you because it gives you energy and makes you feel happy.

Reflection
Our health is very important – if we lose it then, even if we had all the money in the world, we wouldn't be able to enjoy life. Keeping healthy and fit is fun as well as being the best thing for us. If we keep healthy then we will be able to have more energy and strength to take pleasure in the world. We should also remember that we are very fortunate to be able to have lots of food, clean water and places to play and keep ourselves fit. There are lots of children in the world who don't have those opportunities.

Prayer
Lord God,
Thank you for all the things you have provided for us to enjoy good health. Thank you for our bodies and minds that can give us so much enjoyment in the world you have created. Please help us not take our health for granted and to look after ourselves as we grow up. Please help us to remember those who are not as fortunate as us and who don't have clean water and good food.
Amen.

18 We're all Special (Image)

Objective
To promote a healthy and positive self-image for children.

Links
Citizenship
1b: to recognise their worth as individuals by identifying positive things about themselves and their achievements

Props
A box with a lid which has a mirror inside *(perhaps a jewellery box)*.
Some music to play whilst the box is being passed round.

Introduction

Have you seen the box I've brought in today? If I let you look in it, you'll see something so special, something so absolutely wonderful that you'll never forget it. Hands up who wants to have a look inside my box? *(Hopefully all will raise their hands!)*

A very special image
Now, I'm going to open this before I pass it to the first person – very slowly. I'm going to put it very near my face so I can look inside it but someone next to me won't be able to see. Are you ready? I'm opening it very, very slowly *(let out a gasp)*. That's fantastic! It's amazing! I know there's only one like that in the whole world! Any ideas what it might be? *(Invite responses, hopefully none will guess yet that it's their reflection but, if they do, don't give it away!)*

Now, which row shall I start with? *(Choose a row or child.)* I'll start here – now I'm going to give you the box first and, when you've opened it very, very slowly and seen what's inside, you MUSTN'T say what it is. Just close the box very carefully and pass it to the next person. Do you think you can do that? Great! Let's start then. *(Supervise passing the box, ensuring that no child sees the mirror inside until it's their turn – this will obviously take a few minutes! When all the children have seen their image, take the box back.)*

Now, who can tell me what they saw? *(Invite responses and wait for a child to say me, rather than a mirror, or if they do just say the mirror – ask who they saw in the mirror!)* That's right, you saw yourself! When each one of us opened the box, we saw ourselves. We are all, each one of us, very, very special. There is no-one like us in the whole world! Each one of us is unique – who can tell me what unique means? *(the only one)* Well done! Can I have a volunteer please? *(Choose a child.)* Now, did you know *(talking to child)* that no-one else looks like you, no-one else thinks like you and no-one else can do all the things that you can do! You are very special. *(Ask child to sit down.)*

And it's not only X I'm talking about – I'm talking about every single one of you; and me as well! Isn't it wonderful to think that you, and me, are so special? Who can tell me something they're good at? *(Invite responses and praise children that offer replies.)* That is terrific *(offer something you're good at)* – what a talented lot we are!

INTERACTIVE FOLLOW-UP

Questions
1) Who thought there was going to be something different in the box? *(Invite suggestions.)*
2) Who was surprised?
3) Who can remember what unique means? *(the only one)*
4) Why is each one of us unique? *(No-one else looks like us, sounds like us, can do the things we do or thinks like us.)*

Getting the message
Sometimes when we get upset, or if someone is nasty to us, it's easy to think that we don't matter. But we do! Always remember how important and special you are.

Learning more
We're all unique but we're all humans too. Our bodies are really interesting!

Did you know:
- That the highest recorded human sneeze is 102 miles per hour – that's faster than the speed of some trains!
- When you are a child, your heart is about the size of an adult fist; when you are an adult, it's the size of two fists.
- When you smile, you exercise about 30 muscles.
- It is impossible to lick your elbow.
- You use 200 muscles to take one step.
- Now, everyone blink! *(Spend a minute or two with everybody blinking.)* Did you know that we all blink about 10,000 times each day! That's a lot of blinks!

Non-interactive Follow-up

Summary
- In the box was something so amazing and so special that each of the children would never forget it.
- Each one of us is unique, or the only one.
- Nobody can do the things we do, no-one else looks like us, no-one else sounds like us.
- We are all special.

Reflection
When you are fed-up or feeling a bit sad, look around you at all the other people you can see and notice all the different things about them. Then remember that you, too, are different. That there has never been anyone like you and there never will be again! Doesn't that make you feel special?

Prayer
Lord God,
Thank you that you made each one of us to be different. Thank you that we all have different talents and gifts to enjoy life and to serve you. Thank you that we are all special.
Amen.

19 LOOKING AFTER THE ENVIRONMENT
Litter Bug

Objective
To raise children's awareness of their responsibility to look after the environment by putting litter in bins or by recycling it.

Links
Citizenship
2b: why and how rules are made and enforced
2c: to realise the consequences of anti-social behaviour
4a: that their actions affect themselves and others

Geography
5a: recognise how people can improve the environment

Props
A carrier bag with various things that you can take out and then throw on the floor as litter. An insect-type puppet labelled 'anti-litter bug' (this can be very simple, to be used as a tool for the story).

INTRODUCTION

Good morning, I went shopping before I came to school today. It's usually the best time because it's not so busy. Anyway, I got these for my lunch. I'm just going to take all the paper off and put it in the fridge. *(Get various things out, open them and drop the packaging paper and rubbish onto the floor as you speak – suggest biscuit box, sweet wrapper, sandwich wrapper, whatever you want! Walk off to one side and leave all the rubbish on the floor. Children are bound to react!)* What's the matter? Have I done something? *(Produce puppet at this point and enter a dialogue.)*

Puppet: I'll say you have. What do you think you're doing?
You: What do you mean?
Puppet: Well, look at all that rubbish, aren't you going to pick it up?
You: Well, I wasn't going to – someone else can do that, can't they?
Puppet: *(make an appalled sound)* Well, what do you think of that, children? Isn't that absolutely the naughtiest thing you've ever heard?
You: Who are you, anyway?
Puppet: I'm the anti-litter bug and I think you need to listen to this story.
You: Oh, alright then - I'm all ears! *(Use puppet to tell the story.)*

Story: Joe meets the anti-litter bug

Joe loved eating food outside – you name it, he ate it. Burgers, sausage rolls, sweets. Now that's all very well, lots of people like eating outside. But Joe and his family not only ate outside, they left all their rubbish wherever they ate it. Their garden was piled high with rubbish; if you walked along behind them in the street, you'd know where they were going *(and where they'd been)* because they left a trail of rubbish behind them. Joe's mum and dad had never been taught that you put litter in the bin, so of course Joe didn't either.

One day, Joe was walking along the street, munching on a packet of chocolate éclairs. Every time he ate one, he dropped the wrapper on the floor. He was just about to eat his sixth éclair, when he heard a voice behind him. 'Excuse me,' the voice said, 'I think you'd better pick that up!' Joe turned round and couldn't see anyone, so he carried on. 'I said EXCUSE ME, I THINK YOU'D BETTER PICK THAT UP!' Joe looked all around him and then saw something sitting on his shoulder – it fluttered round to the front of him and Joe could see clearly that it was a brightly coloured bug with ANTI-LITTER BUG written on its front. *(That's me!)*

'Were you talking to me?' asked Joe politely.

'I certainly was,' said the anti-litter bug. 'What do you think you're doing – don't you know you should put all your rubbish into bins? Or, even better, recycle it?'

Joe looked confused. 'No I didn't. I'm sorry. Will you show me?'

'I most certainly will,' said the anti litter-bug. Come with me.' So off they went and the anti-litter bug showed Joe where all the rubbish bins were in his town and in his school. He showed him where the recycling centres were so that he and his family could take things like paper, glass and aluminium cans to be recycled. What does recycling mean? *(rubbish that can be made into something else)* He showed him lots of people who put litter in the correct place. 'You see, Joe,' said the anti-litter bug, 'getting rid of rubbish is your responsibility. If you don't put litter in the right place – what a mess it causes. Not only that, it can block drains and cause disease because nasty things like rats can come along. If people leave lots of litter, it makes more litter because people think it doesn't matter and that someone else will clear up for them!'

'I didn't know you could do this,' said Joe excitedly. 'I'm going straight back to tell mum and dad!'

'That's great,' said the anti-litter bug. And that's what Joe did, and now all his family know that the correct place for litter is in bins or at the recycling centre. *(Puppet addresses the children at this point.)* Did you know that? *(Children should respond!)*

Well, thank you anti-litter bug – I'm really sorry! I'll go and clear that mess up right now! *(Pick up all the rubbish from the floor.)*

INTERACTIVE FOLLOW-UP

Questions
1) What did you think when all that rubbish was going on the floor? *(Invite responses.)*
2) What did Joe and his family like doing? *(eating outside)*
3) What did Joe and his family do that was wrong? *(They left rubbish everywhere.)*
4) Why did they do that? *(They didn't think it was their problem and no-one had taught them it was wrong.)*
5) Who turned up to teach him what to do? *(the anti-litter bug)*
6) What did the anti-litter bug teach Joe? *(That it was wrong to leave litter everywhere. That it should be put in bins or taken to recycling centres.)*
7) What did Joe think would happen to all his rubbish? *(Somebody else would clear up after him.)*
8) If lots of rubbish is left everywhere, what happens? *(It makes a mess and causes disease. It also makes more litter because people think it's OK to leave it there.)*

Getting the message – what can I do about it?
Did you know that millions of pounds are spent each year by the government to tidy up our streets? Some people really don't think that litter is their problem and, if they think that, then they don't care very much about their community! If everyone were to put litter in the right place, all that money could be saved and spent on something else! If you never drop litter, that shows that you care for the people and the environment in your community. If you recycle it as well, then you're a real star.

Learning more
Did you also know that, if you drop litter, you're breaking the law? Once children get to 13 years old *(which is a while away yet, but you might have brothers and sisters that age)*, the police can arrest anyone that drops litter. People have been fined up to £2,000! Everyone should recycle litter when they can – there are loads of recycling centres now – there's really no excuse. If you want to find out more about recycling, there are lots of websites that can tell you about it, one is (www.recyclenow.co.uk).

NON-INTERACTIVE FOLLOW-UP

Summary
- Everyone is responsible for disposing of their own litter.
- Joe and his family had never been taught that they should put litter in bins or recycle.
- Joe thought someone else would pick up his litter for him.
- The anti-litter bug showed Joe the correct way to get rid of rubbish and told him it was his responsibility.
- Millions of pounds are spent each year on tidying up the country.
- It is a criminal offence to drop litter after the age of 13.
- There are lots of recycling centres now for people to recycle their rubbish.

Reflection
Litter looks awful and causes disease. Be careful if you see litter in the streets – if you pick it up there could be dangerous things like glass, so always ask an adult to put it in the bin for you. We all want to live in a clean environment – putting our litter in the right place is a big help in keeping our communities tidy and healthy.

Prayer
Lord God,
Help us all to look after our communities by putting litter in the right place. Help us to remember to recycle as well so that we can help to stop pollution.
Amen.

20 Law and Order

Objective
For children to understand the necessity of having a society based on the principles of law and order in order for it to be cohesive and to function effectively.

Links
Citizenship
2b: why and how rules and laws are made and enforced

Props
A few packed lunch boxes with some food items in, e.g. crisps, chocolate, drink cartons, apples.

Introduction

Who brings a packed lunch to school? What are your favourite things to eat in your packed lunch? *(Invite responses, then show packed lunch boxes and take items out.)* What about this, or this? How would you feel if someone came and took your favourite snack out of your packed lunch box? This is a story about a school where some things started to go missing – particularly from packed lunch boxes…

Story: The case of the missing chocolate
Miss Jury was looking a bit stern. All the children were wondering what she was going to say. 'Children,' she began, 'I'm afraid I'm a little anxious this morning. For the third time this week, I've had a child come to me and say that something has gone missing from their packed lunch box.' All the children looked at each other. 'Now, I'm sure there is an explanation. But I want you all to tell me if you see or hear anything suspicious, or if something has been taken from your lunch box. Now it's time for play. Everyone line up.'

The children lined up and got their snacks out of their packed lunch boxes or bags as they went out of the classroom. Ben and Charlie began talking to each other in low voices. 'Did you see Lewis sneaking out of the classroom at playtime yesterday?' asked Ben.

'Yes I did,' said Charlie. 'And he was carrying some chocolate.'

'Do you think,' began Ben.

'I don't know,' said Charlie. 'But I think we'd better keep a look out.' They rushed off into the playground and started to play tag. As Charlie was running round the corner, he saw Lewis going inside the school. He turned back and ran to Ben. 'I've just seen Lewis going into school round the back where the bins are,' he gasped. 'There's no teacher on duty round there.'

'Right,' said Ben. 'Let's go.' They crept in the back entrance, just in time to see Lewis opening a packed lunch box and putting his hand inside.

'Go and get Miss Jury, Ben' whispered Charlie. Ben ran off and Charlie went silently through the door. 'Lewis,' said Charlie. 'What are you doing?'

Lewis jumped and turned round. He had flushed dark red. 'I... I...' he stuttered. He was holding a chocolate bar.

Then they heard another voice. 'Thank you, Charlie,' said Miss Jury. 'You can go back out to play.' Charlie hesitated, then did as he was told. 'Well, Lewis,' said Miss Jury. 'Is that your chocolate?'

Lewis was silent for a while. 'No, Miss,' he mumbled.

'In that case, why is it in your hand?' asked Miss Jury.

'I...' began Lewis, then stopped. He seemed to want to continue.

'Go on, Lewis,' said Miss Jury gently.

'Well, Miss. Every day all the other children have snacks and my mum, she can't afford to give me any chocolate, and... well...'

'So you've been taking chocolate that belongs to other children?' asked Miss Jury.

'Yes, Miss,' said Lewis. He was very ashamed.

'Well, Lewis, just because you haven't got something, it doesn't mean that you can take it from others. That's stealing. Do you understand?'

'Yes, Miss.'

'Lewis, if you promise never to do this again, this will be the end of the matter.' Lewis looked at her, amazed.

'But, Miss, Ben and Charlie – they saw...'

Miss Jury looked at Lewis and said, 'I'll talk to them, don't worry.'

'Thank you, Miss Jury. I'll never do it again,' said Lewis. He was very relieved.

The next day, when the children were going out to play, Ben called Lewis over and said to him, 'Come and play with us, Lewis. I've got some chocolate we can all share.' And they did.

INTERACTIVE FOLLOW-UP

Questions
1) Why was Miss Jury looking stern? *(because things had been taken from packed lunch boxes)*
2) What did she ask the children to do? *(look out for anything suspicious)*
3) What had Ben and Charlie noticed the day before? *(Lewis was sneaking out of the classroom with a bar of chocolate.)*
4) What happened when Charlie and Ben were playing tag? *(Charlie saw Lewis going into school by the back entrance where there was no teacher on duty.)*
5) What did he do? *(He went and got Ben.)*
6) What happened next? *(They saw Lewis taking some chocolate, so Ben went and got Miss Jury. Charlie asked Lewis what he was doing and then Miss Jury told them to go.)*
7) Why did Lewis take the chocolate? *(because his mum couldn't afford to give him a snack to take to school)*
8) What did Miss Jury say to him? *(That he was stealing. She said that, if it never happened again, the matter would be closed.)*
9) What happened the next day? *(Ben and Charlie offered to share their chocolate with Lewis.)*
10) How do you think Lewis felt when he was caught? *(frightened, embarrassed, worried)*
11) What did Miss Jury say that he had been doing? *(stealing)*
12) Why is stealing wrong? *(You should never take things that don't belong to you and it's against the law.)*
13) Why do you think Ben and Charlie offered to share with Lewis? *(They were being kind and realised that Lewis' family didn't have much money.)*

Getting the message – what can I do about it?
Sometimes we all want things that other people have got but stealing them is no answer. Imagine how you would feel if someone stole something of yours? Stealing is always wrong and it is against the law. When people do something that is against the law, they have to know that they will be in trouble if they are caught. You can make sure that you never break the law and you can, like Ben and Charlie, look out for people that do. If you see anybody taking anything that you know isn't theirs, you must tell your teacher.

Learning more
Grown-ups and children have to obey rules. Rules are necessary so that our homes, schools, places of work and our country run smoothly.

NON-INTERACTIVE FOLLOW-UP

Summary
- Miss Jury was looking stern because items had gone missing from packed lunch boxes.
- She asked the children to look out for anything suspicious.
- Ben and Charlie had seen Lewis sneaking out of the classroom the day before with a bar of chocolate.
- Charlie saw Lewis going into school where there was no teacher on duty.
- He found Ben and they followed Lewis who they saw taking some chocolate.
- They both went and found Miss Jury who confronted Lewis.
- He said that he had taken the chocolate because his mum couldn't afford to buy him a snack to bring to school.
- Miss Jury told him that he had been stealing but, if he promised never to do it again, then the matter would be closed.
- Ben and Charlie offered to share their snacks with Lewis the next day.
- Taking things from other people is stealing and it is against the law.

Reflection
As well as our teachers and parents protecting us, the police are there to protect us from people who do wrong things. It is good that we have people whose jobs are to make sure that people who do things like stealing are caught.

Prayer
Lord God,
Thank you that we have rules and laws to protect us. Thank you for all the people who make sure that rules are obeyed. Help us to always know the difference between right and wrong. Amen.

21 Global Warming

Objective
To help children reflect on the issue of global warming and to give them information to enable them to make informed choices about how they can help improve the environment.

Links
Citizenship
2a: to research, discuss and debate topical issues, problems and events
2h: to recognise the role of voluntary, community and pressure groups
2j: resources can be allocated in different ways and that these economic choices affect individuals, communities and the sustainability of the environment

Props
3 hats and 3 raincoats.
1 pair of sunglasses.
3 magnifying glasses.
Two old mobile phones.
OHP, transparency and pens (if not using whiteboard).
Images of polar ice cap melting (optional).

Introduction

Can I have three volunteers please? *(Choose 3 children and give them the raincoats and hats; give one the mobile and the sunglasses and other mobile to different children. Explain that they are detectives and they've got to walk around with their magnifying glasses looking for clues and act out the things that you say. One of them is Detective Supercool [he/she has the sunglasses] and waits at the side until he/she is called.)*

Detective Cool and Detective Cooler were getting confused. It was getting hotter. The winters were getting warmer and shorter and the summers were getting hotter and longer. They looked for clues everywhere, but they couldn't find anything. They scratched their heads and looked puzzled. Meanwhile, it was getting even hotter – so they took off their coats and hats and puzzled again. It was time to get to the bottom of things – then they had an idea! It was time to call Detective Supercool – he'd know what to do! *(Tell one child to call Detective Supercool on the mobile.)* 'Don't worry, Cool,' said Cooler. 'He's on his way!' *(Tell Detective Supercool to leap on dramatically.)*

'And here he is!' *(Ask Detectives Cool and Cooler to sit down, ask Detective Supercool to stay there and look clever.)*

What's going on?
Detective Supercool certainly looks as though he's got all the answers, doesn't he? *(Detective Supercool nods.)* Who's heard of something called global warming?

(Invite responses.) That's right, global warming simply means that the Earth is getting warmer. So, why is that? Detective Cool will need to look everywhere on the Earth to find out! Isn't that right, Detective Supercool? *(Nods again.)* But he really needs to explain a few things first. Can I help you do that? *(Nods again.)*

Hands up who's got a greenhouse at home? It gets hot in there, doesn't it? Well, the Earth is kind of similar to a greenhouse. There are special gases in the Earth's atmosphere which are actually called greenhouse gases – they help make the Earth warm enough for us, animals and plants to live. But, things people (and that means you and me) are doing, like using electricity, heating our homes, driving cars, cutting down trees and making things in factories, are putting extra greenhouse gases into the air. Because we've got extra gases in the Earth's atmosphere now, they are making the Earth get warmer. There are too many of them! All these things that we've been doing are now starting to make a bigger difference. They are making the climate, or our weather, do different things – like more storms, flooding and more heat. Detective Supercool knows all this and we're going to tell you how you can help stop the Earth getting hotter in a bit, aren't we, Detective Supercool? *(Nods again.)*

INTERACTIVE FOLLOW-UP

Questions

- What was Detective Cool and Detective Cooler worried about? *(They were getting too hot!)*
- Who did they call to come and help them find out about it? *(Detective Supercool)*
- What does global warming mean? *(the Earth's getting hotter)*
- What do the greenhouse gases in the Earth's atmosphere do? *(keep the Earth warm enough for humans, animals and plants to live)*
- What kinds of things are we doing that make too many greenhouse gases? *(driving, using electricity, heating our homes, cutting down trees, factories)*
- What effect are the greenhouse gases having on our weather? *(storms, flooding, higher temperatures)*
- Do you think Detective Supercool knows it all?!

Getting the message – what can I do about it?

Detective Supercool says there is a lot you can do about it! *(Nods!)* Let's make a little list. *(If using a whiteboard, you could perhaps write the list up here, or use an OHP.)* Does anyone have any ideas? *(Invite responses and write appropriate actions; the finished article should be along the following lines:)*

- Walk and cycle more, use cars less.
- Switch off electrical appliances when not in use.
- Plant more trees.
- Wear more clothes rather than turning up the heat when it's cold.

That's great! Thank you, Detective Supercool, you've been a great help. I'm sure we all know about global warming now and we know how we can help. *(Ask Detective Supercool to sit down.)*

Learning more

It's not just at home we can think about our actions – at school we use lots of electricity. So be alert! If you see computers left on at the end of the day – remind your teacher to switch them off! Make sure the lights are turned off when your class isn't in the classroom. Check whether the school is using low-energy light bulbs! Make yourself a nuisance to your teachers and tell them to walk, bike or catch a train or bus to school! If you want to find out more, visit some websites on global warming which will give you more information. There are loads! Just type in global warming on a search and take your pick. It's a good idea to type kids as well so that you get sites for children.

NON-INTERACTIVE FOLLOW-UP

Summary
- Detectives Cool and Cooler were worried that the Earth was getting hotter.
- They called Detective Supercool to come and explain things to them!
- The Earth's atmosphere is like a greenhouse. It has gases which keep the Earth warm enough for humans, plants and animals.
- The Earth is producing too many greenhouse gases, which is making the Earth hotter and that is affecting our climate.
- The extra greenhouse gases are produced from cars, heating, electricity, fewer trees and factories.
- We can help by switching electrical appliances off when we're not using them, using our cars less, planting more trees and wearing more clothes when it's cold instead of turning the heating up.

Reflection

We all live on the Earth, so we must all take action to help stop global warming. That means really thinking about our daily lives and how we can change. If you feel strongly, talk to your mums and dads about how you as a family can make a difference.

Prayer

Lord God,
Thank you for the Earth and all the things you have provided for us. We know that we can all help to make a difference to global warming. Help us to remember to switch lights and electrical things off when we are not using them and to walk and cycle whenever we can.
Amen.

22 Need and Want

Objective
For children to be aware of the difference between wants and needs and to understand the value of saving and not getting into debt through borrowing.

Links
Citizenship
1f: to look after their money and realise that future wants and needs may be met through saving

Props
2 PE mats put at either side of the hall.

INTRODUCTION

Who watches telly adverts? *(Invite responses.)* What are adverts for? *(Trying to make you (or your mums and dads) buy things.)* Have you ever badgered your mums and dads for something so much that they've eventually bought you it? Or have you really wanted to buy something with your pocket money but you haven't got quite enough, so you've asked your mum and dad to lend you some? *(Invite responses.)* Let's listen to a story about two people who wanted something, but they didn't have enough money to do it!

Story: More room!
Can I have some volunteers please? *(Choose two children to be a husband and wife, one person to be the Very Wise Man; two children to be sheep, two to be pigs, two to be cows and two to be hens – if you've got a big PE mat, you might need to have some more animals! Ask another child to bang on a drum for sound effects when the husband and wife knock on the Very Wise Man's door. Explain to children that you're going to read the story and they have to act it out as you're speaking. Ask the man and wife to stand on one mat and the Very Wise Man to stand on the other. All the animals should wait at the side until it's their turn to get on the mat!)*

Once upon a time, there was a husband and wife who lived on a farm but they were very unhappy. They thought their house was too small. They had enough money to buy food and all the things they needed, but they didn't have enough money to build a bigger house. BUT they really wanted a bigger house. So they decided they would go to the Very Wise Man and ask him if they could borrow some money from him to build a bigger house. They thought, if they borrowed some money, they could then pay it back a bit at a time (even though they couldn't really afford it). So off they went and knocked on the Very Wise Man's door. Knock! Knock! Knock! *(Have drum sound effects here.)*

The Very Wise Man opened the door and said, 'Hello, can I help you?'

The husband and wife said, 'Yes please. Our house is too small and we'd like to borrow some money to build a bigger one.' The Very Wise Man thought for a moment *(ask child to adopt a thinking pose)* and said, 'Hmm. Go back and get two cows from your farm and bring them into the house with you.' The husband and wife looked at each other and thought that was a very strange thing to say but, because the Very Wise Man was so wise, they went back and brought two cows into the house. *(Children get the two children who are cows and take them onto their mat.)*

After a while they thought to themselves, 'This is no good. We'll have to go back and see the Very Wise Man again.' So off they went, and knocked on The Very Wise Man's door. Knock! Knock! Knock! *(Sound effects.)*

The Very Wise Man opened the door and said, 'Hello, can I help you?'

The husband and wife said, 'Yes please. Our house is definitely too small – especially with the cows. Can we borrow some money to build a bigger house please?'

The Very Wise Man thought again for a moment and said, 'Go back and get two pigs to live in the house with you.' The husband and wife looked at each other again, and thought this was even stranger but, because the Very Wise Man was so wise, they did as he said. Back they went and got two pigs from the farm to live in the house. *(Children get the two pigs and bring them onto the mat with them.)*

After a while, they thought, 'This is no good. It's far too cramped in here. We'll have to go and see the Very Wise Man again.' So off they went and knocked on the Very Wise Man's door. Knock! Knock! Knock! *(Sound effects.)*

'Hello,' said the Very Wise Man. 'Can I help you?'

'You certainly can,' said the husband and wife. 'Our house is too small, and getting smaller by the minute! Can we borrow some money to build a bigger house please?'

Again the Very Wise Man thought, then he said. 'Well, I think you should go back to your farm and get two sheep and take them into the house to live with you.' The husband and wife were amazed! But they knew that the Very Wise Man was very wise and so they did as he said. *(Children get the two sheep and take them back to the mat.)*

After a while, the husband and wife said, 'This is too much! We'll have to go back and see him again.' So they did, they knocked on the door. Knock! Knock! Knock! *(Sound effects!)*

The Very Wise Man answered again. 'Hello,' he said, very pleasantly, 'Can I help you?'

'Yes, you jolly well can,' said the husband and wife. 'Please can we borrow some money to build a bigger house? It's absolutely heaving now!'

'Well,' said the Very Wise Man, looking at them thoughtfully. 'I think you should go back to your farm and get two hens to take into the house with you.' The husband and wife were astonished! More animals! But, because the Very Wise Man was so wise, they agreed. So back they went and got the hens. *(Husband and wife get the hens and take them to the mat.)* When the hens were in the house too they all jostled around trying to find some space.

Eventually the husband and wife thought, 'We MUST get a house with more room. We'll go back to the Very Wise Man once more and see what he says.' So they trekked back to the Very Wise Man's house and knocked on the door. Knock! Knock! Knock! *(Sound effects again!)*

The Very Wise Man opened the door and said, 'Don't tell me. You want to borrow some money to build a bigger house?'

The husband and wife were very happy, gave the Very Wise Man a big smile and said, 'Yes Please!'

The Very Wise Man looked thoughtful (as usual!) and then he said, 'Go back to your house and put all the animals back onto the farmland.' The husband and wife stopped smiling immediately and looked at each other sadly. But, because the Very Wise Man was so wise, they did as he said and went back and put all the animals back onto the farm. *(Husband and wife go back to their mat and lead the animals off onto the 'farm'.)* Then they trudged back to their house, feeling very sad. When they got to their house, they walked in and then stopped and looked around – what a wonderful big house they had! They couldn't believe how much room there was.

'Aren't we lucky to have such a big house,' they said to each other. 'Why on earth did we think we needed somewhere bigger?'

INTERACTIVE FOLLOW-UP

Questions
1) Hands up if you think the Very Wise Man was very wise!
2) Why do you think he told the husband and wife to put all those animals in their house? *(So they would appreciate the space they had and realise they didn't really need anywhere bigger.)*
3) Did the husband and wife need a bigger house or want a bigger house? *(want)*
4) Can anyone tell me the difference between wanting something and needing something? *(Needs are things that are essential to survive – e.g. food, drink, somewhere to live; wants are extras that aren't necessary.)*
5) Apart from them realising the house was big enough for them, what else do you think the husband and wife might be grateful to the Very Wise Man for? *(They didn't have to borrow any money.)*
6) If they had borrowed some money, what would they have had to do? *(Pay the money back a little bit at a time.)*
7) Is it a good idea to borrow money if you haven't got much in the first place? *(No, because you have to pay it back and that can be difficult because you can't afford to buy the things you need.)*

Getting the message – what can I do about it?
Sometimes we all want things that we can't have or haven't got enough money to buy. But, when we really think about it, mostly those things aren't what we need, they're what we want. And there's a big difference. What kind of things do we need? *(Food, water, somewhere to live, clothes, things to keep us warm.)* What are the things we want? *(More toys, clothes, nice holidays.)* Of course, it's lovely to have extra things sometimes and we all want those things sometimes. But it's not

really a good idea to borrow in order to get them. Hands up if you ever get some birthday money or Christmas money to spend on yourself? I'm sure you do and that's lovely. Hands up if you ever save any money if you're given it as a treat? That's great. It's always a good idea to save money so that, if there is something you want, or if you decide to buy your mums or dads or grannies, grandpas, brothers and sisters a nice present for their birthday or Christmas, then you've got it to spend! And it's a really nice feeling when you give somebody something – even better than when you get a present yourself!

Learning more

The husband and wife learnt a valuable lesson after they put the animals back onto the farm. Before the house was so crowded, they thought they didn't have enough room and wanted more. But, after having to live in cramped conditions for a while, they learnt to appreciate what they had, rather than wanting more when they couldn't afford it.

NON-INTERACTIVE FOLLOW-UP

Summary

- The husband and wife thought their house was too small, so they decided to ask the Very Wise Man if they could borrow some money.
- The wise man told them to put cows, pigs, sheep and hens in the house each time they went to him to ask for money.
- The husband and wife were very surprised but did as the Very Wise Man told them to.
- The last time the husband and wife went to see the Very Wise Man, he told them to put all the animals back into the fields
- When they returned to the house, they realised that their house wasn't small after all.
- They thought they needed more room but they actually wanted more room.
- Needs are things that are essential (like food, water, clothes, somewhere to live); wants are extra things, which are not necessary (like more toys, extra clothes, extra anything!).

Reflection

When we see things advertised on television or anywhere, it's easy to be fooled into thinking that we actually need those things. Very often they are people who are trying to persuade us to spend money in order to make other people rich! It is important to know the difference between wanting things and needing things in order to spend and save our money wisely.

Prayer

Lord God,
Thank you for all the things that we have and for all the things you have provided. Help us in the future to understand the difference between wanting things and needing things so that we can use our money wisely.
Amen.

23 Homelessness

Objective
To understand what homelessness is, what causes it and how people can help the homeless.

Links
Citizenship
2c: to realise that people and other living things have needs, and that they have responsibilities to meet them

5g: consider social and moral dilemmas that they come across in everyday life

Props
No props are needed but this assembly is presented in the form of a reading for five pupils, so five copies of the script will need to be made. The children chosen to read aloud the five parts *(a narrator plus homeless characters A, B, C, D)* should be good readers from Y1 or Y2 who have the confidence to speak aloud before an audience. They should have an opportunity to practise too.

Introduction

Today's assembly is all about a group of people who need a lot of help. Five people are going to help me to tell their story.

Reading: Please help us
Narrator: If you walk on the streets of any big city for long, you will see people like this:

A: I don't know where I am going to sleep tonight.

B: I have no money and no food and no shelter.

C: I lost my job and had to leave my family because I have problems.

D: I have no family or friends – I am cold and lonely.

All: We are homeless – please help us.

A: I cannot afford to buy or rent a house.

B: I am not well so I cannot work to earn money.

C: I cannot cope with things on my own.

D: I have been in trouble with the police – no one likes me.

All: We are homeless – please help us.

A: It is so cold and wet on the streets at night – please give me a blanket.

B: I hate sleeping among cardboard boxes in doorways – please give me shelter.

C: I need proper food and clean clothes – please help me to find them.

D: I feel poorly all the time – please tell me where there is somewhere I can live.

All: We are homeless – please help us.

Teacher: There are homeless people on the streets of every city around the world. They have no homes to go to and some of them are only children too.

Is anybody helping these people? Yes, charity organisations like the Salvation Army do lots of things to help homeless people:
- They provide shelters with beds.
- They give out blankets and hot food.
- They talk to people who need help.
- They help homeless people to find proper homes.

One way that you can help is to give money to charities like this so that they can help even more homeless people.

INTERACTIVE FOLLOW-UP

Questions
1) What are homeless people? *(people who have no home of their own)*
2) Where do most homeless people live? *(in cities)*
3) Why do some people become homeless? *(They lose their job or they become ill or get into trouble – there are many reasons.)*
4) Who helps homeless people? *(Charities such as the Salvation Army who provide shelters and much more. Anyone who raises money for these charities is helping homeless people too.)*

Getting the message
Call out yes or no for each statement:
- Everyone has a home.
- Some people like having no home.
- Homeless people are found in countries all over the world.
- Houses are cheap to buy.
- Homeless people need help to find somewhere to live.
- Some charities help homeless people.

Briefly discuss why people become homeless, making it clear to children that reasons are often quite complicated and sometimes it's not anybody's fault. Explain that many homeless people do eventually find homes.

Learning more
The government does try to help homeless people but not always as well as it could. Ask the children for ideas – what would they do to help the homeless if they were Prime Minister? In some countries, there are street children who live on the streets and sleep rough and live by begging or crime. Discuss what can be done to help these children.

Non-Interactive Follow-up

Summary
- There are lots of people around the world who have no home.
- These people are called homeless people.
- They are people who are poor and needy.
- They become homeless for many reasons, e.g. they lose their job or they become ill or get into trouble.
- Homeless people often have to sleep rough on the streets where they get hungry and cold and often become ill.
- Charities such as the Salvation Army help the homeless in lots of ways, e.g. by providing shelters.
- We can help the homeless by giving money to charities such as the Salvation Army.

Reflection

Having no home makes people sad. Everyone needs a home. Think about people who roam the streets and sleep in doorways. They need lots of help. Remember, when you see a charity box for the homeless or someone collecting money – try to give something.

Prayer

Dear Lord,
Thank you for our homes wherever we live. Thank you that we have somewhere warm and safe to go. Please help those people who are not so lucky. Please help the homeless to find homes and help the charity workers who make their lives better.
Amen.

24 Water

Objective
To learn about the importance of water and to understand how difficult it is to obtain for some people around the world.

Links
PSHE/Citizenship
4c: to identify and respect the differences and similarities between people
5g: consider social and moral dilemmas that they come across in everyday life

Props
A glass of water.

Introduction

What's in this glass? Water of course! How do we get water? Not everyone gets it from a tap, as you'll find out in this story.

Story: Abdou and Alex
'Wake up, Alex, it's eight o'clock,' said Alex's dad. 'Time for your shower.'
Alex pulled himself out of bed and walked across the landing to the bathroom. Alex lived in Cardiff, which is a city in Wales.

A long, long way away, many thousands of miles across the sea, another seven year-old boy was woken up by his mum. His name was Abdou. 'Come on Abdou, it's late. You need to go and get some water.' Abdou stood up and rubbed his eyes. He pulled on some clothes and stepped outside to find the empty plastic basin he needed. Then, with his nine year-old sister, Jama, he set off to walk half a mile to the river to collect water to have a wash. Abdou lived in a village in Senegal in Africa.

Alex had a big bowl of cereal for breakfast. His dad made him a glass of orange squash. He filled the glass at the cold tap and passed it to Alex. 'Make sure that you drink plenty today, Alex.' Alex nodded.

In Abdou's village, Abdou and his sister arrived back at the house, each carrying a heavy basin of water. It had taken them thirty minutes. Abdou's mother poured some of the water into a metal saucepan and put it over a fire to boil. Abdou used the rest to have a wash. He was thirsty and wanted to have a drink but the water had to be boiled. 'Why do we have to boil the water before we drink it?' asked Abdou.

'This river water has germs in it which can give us bad diseases. Boiling kills them and makes it safe to drink,' said his mum. Abdou groaned – he would have to wait.

At Alex's house, his father put the washing machine on and then went outside to wash his car. He attached a hose to the outside tap and switched it on. Alex came out and his dad sprayed him with water. It was fun. Alex helped with the washing up after this. They used lots of water from the hot tap.

In Africa, Abdou finally got his drink once the water had cooled down. He then had some corn porridge for breakfast. After this, he went out to play football then walked down to the river again to help his mum carry the clothes for washing. At the river, Abdou's mum washed his clothes while Abdou paddled in the shallow part nearby. Then he watched a farmer bring his cows to the river for a drink. Abdou carried more water home for cooking when the washing was done.

Back in England, Alex used lots more water: flushing the toilet, brushing his teeth, having drinks, washing his hands, watering the garden, washing up the plates after dinner and giving his dog a bath.

Abdou used much less water than Alex. He went to the river three times in all that day and, when he went to bed, he dreamed about what it must be like to live in a village with water pipes and a tap so that you didn't have to walk to the river. It was a wonderful dream.

INTERACTIVE FOLLOW-UP

Questions

1) Where did Alex and Abdou live? *(In Wales and Senegal in Africa.)*
2) How were the two boys' lives different? *(Abdou had no running water in his house and had to go to the river. Everything revolved around getting water for Abdou, whereas Alex used a lot of water by just turning on a tap.)*
3) Why did Abdou have to wait so long for a drink in the morning? *(He had to get water from the river which then had to be boiled to kill bacteria to prevent disease.)*
4) How many things did Alex and his family use water for? *(Washing themselves, making breakfast and other meals, drinking, washing up, cleaning the car, giving the dog a bath, going to the toilet and watering the garden.)*

Getting the message

Water is the most important thing we use, along with air and food. Let's see what you know about water. For each thing I say, put your thumb up if it's true and down if it's not true:
- Every person needs water every day. *(T)*
- All water is alright to drink. *(F)*
- Water is free. *(F)*
- Lots of houses in Africa do have taps and sinks and baths. *(T)*
- Boiling dirty water kills germs in it. *(T)*
- Water in our country can never run out. *(F)*

Some places in Britain have a hosepipe ban every year. What is a hosepipe ban and why do we have them? *(Briefly explain that our water comes from rain and that we all use so much every day that in dry periods it can quickly run out.)*

Learning more

Ask the children to suggest ways that we can save water (or not waste it). Suggestions might include:
- Taking showers instead of baths.
- Turn off the tap when brushing teeth.
- Don't use a hose in the garden.
- Use washing-up water for plants.
- Turn off dripping taps.

Emphasise that it's important for our health to drink a lot of water: at least five glassfuls a day and more in hot weather.

Non-interactive Follow-up

Summary
- Alex is a seven year-old boy who lives in Wales.
- Abdou is the same age – he lives in a village in Senegal in Africa.
- Alex gets his water for washing and drinking and cooking from the tap.
- Abdou has to walk a long way to the river for his water and has to carry it back.
- Abdou's water, unlike Alex's, is not clean – it has to be boiled before it can be drunk.
- Abdou's family's whole life revolves around fetching water from the river.

Reflection

Nearly everybody in our country takes clean water for granted. That means that we're so used to having it available all the time that we forget how important it is. Think about the millions of people around the world like Abdou who don't have taps or pipes or baths or showers or sinks. They have to get their water from rivers and wells, and carry it. Water is heavy to carry and it's often full of germs and dirt. Try to be grateful every time you turn on a tap.

Prayer

Dear Lord,
Thank you for clean fresh clear water. Thank you that we have taps and pipes and showers and baths. Help us to remember those people on the planet who struggle to get water every day and have to carry it and boil it. Help us to find ways to help them to get clean water and help us not to waste our own precious water.
Amen.

25 Keeping Safe in the Sun

Objective
To raise children's awareness of the dangers of exposure to the sun and to inform them of choices they can make to minimise risks to their health.

Links
PSHE/Citizenship
3a how to make simple choices that improve their health and well-being.

Props
2 pairs of sunglasses *(the dafter the better)*.
2 sunhats *(again, the dafter the better)*.
Folding chair.
Bucket and spade and other outside play items – e.g. beach ball, boules.
Carrier bag.
2 packs of sun cream – Factor 20 or suitable for children.
Photocopies of play script for 2 teachers or teaching assistants.

Introduction

Teacher 1: Look at this wonderful weather *(peering as if looking outside)*, I'm off to the beach. *(Picks up folding chair and carrier bag containing book, bucket and spade and other beach toys and marches off.)*

Teacher 2: *(wearing sun hat, sunglasses and carrying sun cream and other carrier bag with spare hat, sunglasses and sun cream)* Oi! Where do you think you're going?

Teacher 1: *(turning round)* Who's that? Oh, it's you. Well, I'm off to the beach – it's such a lovely day – the sun's shining and there isn't a cloud in the sky. I'm going to build lots of sandcastles *(gets out bucket and spade)* and I'm going to sit in the sun and read my book. *(Takes out book to show children – something like the Beano annual or Superman, or a made-up book with a title like 'How to build the best sandcastles in the world'.)*

Teacher 2: Well, you're daft then.

Teacher 1: *(looks hurt)* What do you mean? I'm just going to enjoy myself. You're just jealous because you can't build sandcastles as well as me.

Teacher 2: *(rolls eyes and says to children)* See what I mean? Daft!

Teacher 1: I'm daft? Look at all that gear you're wearing! I suppose you think you look cool!

Teacher 2: I'm not wearing this to look cool. Do you want to know why I'm wearing it?

Teacher 1: Well, I'm absolutely positive you're going to tell me!

Teacher 2: I certainly am. Did you know that it's not good to spend too much time in the sun?

Teacher 1: *(looking interested)* No I didn't. Why not?

Teacher 2: Well, the first reason is that you can get very sunburnt.

Teacher 1: Is that why you're wearing that hat?

Teacher 2: Yep. The hat protects my eyes, ears, face and the back of my neck – they're the places that are particularly prone to getting burnt.

Teacher 1: That's brilliant. A really good idea. There's nothing worse than sunburnt ears! I think I should get one.

Teacher 2: Look no further – I've got a spare. *(bring out spare hat)* What do you think?

Teacher 1: Great! Can I borrow it? *(puts it on)*

Teacher 2: 'Course you can. *(Inspects hat.)* Very nice! Almost as good as mine. Do you like my sunglasses?

Teacher 1: I do actually.

Teacher 2: I do too. I actually think they make me look super cool *(to children)* – what do you think?

Teacher 1: Well, I wouldn't go quite that far. *(winking at children)* But they're OK.

Teacher 2: Well, I'm not wearing them just to look cool (although I know I do). Wearing sunglasses protects my eyes from possible damage from the sun.

Teacher 1: *(looking sad)* I really wish I had some sunglasses.

Teacher 2: Fret not! I just happen to have some in my bag. *(rummages around)* Here!

Teacher 1: Fantastic! *(puts them on)* How do I look?

Teacher 2: Er… great! *(stifles a laugh)*

Teacher 1: Right, now I really am off!

Teacher 2: Wait!

Teacher 1: Now what?

Teacher 2: You've forgotten something else. It's really important to put sun cream on.

Teacher 1: But I haven't got any!

Teacher 2: Never fear, I'm here! *(produces sun cream from bag)*

Teacher 1: You ought to open a shop! Why do I need this, then?

Teacher 2: It's really important to wear sun cream wherever your skin is showing. And, it's got to have a Sun Protection Factor of at least 15 – you just look at the front and it tells you what Factor the cream is. *(Show Factor to the children.)*

Teacher 1: So do I just put it on once? Won't it all come off when I go swimming?

Teacher 2: That's a really good point. You have to put it on about every two hours – even if it's waterproof.

Teacher 1: So am I all set then?

Teacher 2: Do you know, I think you are!

Teacher 1: Great! Hey, why don't you come too? I can teach you how to build ace sandcastles!

Teacher 2: I'll just get my bucket and spade! *(Both exit.)*

INTERACTIVE FOLLOW-UP

Questions

Choose which is the correct answer:

Where was the first teacher going to?
- The cinema
- The beach
- The park

He was going to:
- Build sandcastles
- Make a barbecue
- Go for a bike ride

The second teacher was wearing:
- A sun hat
- Sunglasses
- Sun cream
- All three

Wearing a sun hat:
- Saves you washing your hair
- Saves you combing your hair
- Protects your face, neck, eyes and ears from the sun

Wearing sunglasses:
- Helps you see underwater
- Protects your eyes from being damaged by the sun
- Helps you swim better

Sun cream needs to have a Sun Protection Factor of at least:
- 200
- 3
- 15

Getting the message – what can I do about it?

Although the sun is hot, it's cool! It makes things grow, keeps us warm and gives us something called Vitamin D which gives us strong bones. But we have to be careful because the sun's rays can damage our skin if we don't look after ourselves properly.

You don't need to hide from the sun completely or wrap up like a mummy to protect yourself. But you should take these precautions:

1. Always wear sun cream. Don't forget to put it on places that you might not think of – like the tops of your feet and behind your ears. Make sure you put more on if you've been in the water.
2. Take frequent breaks from the sun by going indoors or moving into the shade. This is especially important between 10:00 in the morning and 4:00 in the afternoon, when the sun's rays are strongest.
3. We need to drink water to stay healthy, especially when it's hot outside. When you're sweating, you lose water that your body needs to work properly. And, if you're playing a sport or running around in the sun, you lose even more water, because you sweat that much more. So drink plenty of water and don't wait until you're thirsty. If you forget and suddenly feel thirsty, start drinking then. There are loads of cool-looking water bottles around, so get one you really like, fill it up and drink up!

Learning more

Some people get sunburnt faster than others because of their colouring. If you have blond or red hair, light-coloured skin and light-coloured eyes, you'll tend to get sunburnt more quickly than someone with dark eyes and skin. That's because you have less melanin. Melanin is a chemical in the skin that protects the skin from sun damage. People with darker skin have more melanin, but even if you have dark hair, dark eyes, or darker-toned skin, you can still get sunburnt. It will just take a little bit longer.

Sunburnt skin looks bad and feels even worse! It can leave you inside feeling sore while everyone else is outside having fun. It increases your chance of getting wrinkly when you get older. And, worst of all, it can lead to skin cancer when you get older. Because getting wrinkles and getting poorly don't happen right away, they can seem like things that could never happen to you. But you still need to be careful.

NON-INTERACTIVE FOLLOW-UP

Summary
- If you go out in the sun, make sure you wear sunglasses, a hat and sun cream.
- Put more sun cream on every couple of hours, especially if you have been in the water.
- Don't go out much between 10 and 4 because that's when the sun's rays are strongest.
- Drink plenty of water to avoid getting dehydrated.
- People with paler hair and skin need to have more protection as they burn more quickly.
- People with darker skin have more melanin in their skin, but they can still get sunburnt – it just takes longer.
- Not looking after yourself in the sun can lead to wrinkly skin and skin cancer in later life.

Reflection
Remember that the good news is that the sun doesn't have to be your enemy if you wear sun cream, drink plenty of water and take regular breaks when you start to feel too hot. And don't forget your hat and sunglasses. Not only do they protect your eyes from the sun, they also make you look cool!

Prayer
Dear Lord,
Thank you for the warmth of the sun and all the things that it provides for us. Help us to remember to look after ourselves when we are playing and not to take unnecessary risks with our health.
Amen.

Badger Publishing Limited
15 Wedgwood Gate, Pin Green Industrial Estate,
Stevenage, Hertfordshire SG1 4SU
Telephone: 01438 356907
Fax: 01438 747015
www.badger-publishing.co.uk
enquiries@badger-publishing.co.uk

Badger Assembly Stories with Global Issues themes
Ages 5–7
ISBN 1 84424 678 7

Text © Sally Maynard, Andy and Barbara Seed 2006
Complete work © Badger Publishing Limited 2006

Once it has been purchased, you may copy this book freely for use in your school. The pages in this book are copyright, but copies may be made without fees or prior permission provided that these copies are used only by the institution which purchased the book. For copying in any other circumstances, prior written consent must be obtained from the publisher.

The right of Sally Maynard, and Andy and Barbara Seed, to be identified as authors of this Work has been asserted by them in accordance with the Copyright, Designs and Patents Act 1988.

Publisher: David Jamieson
Editor: Paul Martin
Designer: Cathy May

For details of the full range of
books and resources from

Badger Publishing

including

- Book Boxes for Early Years, Infants, Juniors and Special Needs
- Badger Guided Reading and book packs for KS1-2
- Badger Nursery Rhymes and Storyteller - for Early Years and KS1
- Full Flight, Dark Flight, First Flight & Rex Jones for reluctant readers
- Brainwaves – non-fiction to get your brain buzzing
- First Facts - non-fiction for infants
- Teaching Writing and Writing Poetry – for Years 1–6
- Expert at… English and Speaking & Listening – Copymaster books
- Delbert's Worksheets and Practice Questions for the KS1-2 Maths SATs
- Badger Maths: Problem Solving Books 1–2
- Badger KS2 Revision Quizzes for English, Maths and Science
- Badger Test Revision Guides for English, Maths and Science
- SATs Practice Papers for English, Maths and Science
- Badger Religious Education – complete course for the primary school
- Badger Geography – complete course for the primary school
- Badger Science – complete course for the primary school
- Badger Comprehension – complete courses for the primary school
- Badger ICT – complete course for the primary school
- Badger Citizenship & PSHE – complete course for the primary school
- Badger French – simple resources for non-specialist teachers
- Basic Background Knowledge – History, Geography
- Badger History for KS1 – big books and teacher books
- Badger Assembly Stories – PSHE, RE and Global Issues – for KS1–2
- Class Act – easy, inspiring cross-curricular drama for KS2

Interactive Whiteboard CD-ROMs
- Badger Comprehension Interactive
- Full Flight Guided Writing

CD versions of many titles also now available

See our full colour Catalogue

available on request
or visit our website www.badger-publishing.co.uk

Contact us at:

Badger Publishing Limited, 15 Wedgwood Gate,
Pin Green Industrial Estate, Stevenage, Hertfordshire SG1 4SU

Telephone: 01438 356907   Fax: 01438 747015

enquiries@badger-publishing.co.uk

**Or visit our showroom and bookshop
at the above address.**